A study in the phenomenon of tongue speaking

GLOSSOLALIA

from God or man?

D1617260

by
JIMMY JIVIDEN

All Scripture Quotations are from the American Standard Version

Star
BIBLE PUBLICATIONS
P.O. BOX 13125
FORT WORTH, TEXAS 76118

ACKNOWLEDGMENTS

I owe many debts for whatever merit this book might have. Scores of individuals have contributed to my understanding of the subject by asking questions and sharing with me the results of their own study. Tom Olbricht, J. W. Roberts, R. L. Roberts, and Paul Faulkner have offered valuable suggestions. Appreciation is extended to Reuel Lemmons who first published a series of my articles on glossolalia in *The Firm Foundation* and has continued to encourage me in my writing. Bill Luttrell, who proofread the manuscript, and my secretaries, Ruby Busby and Rosemary Hays, have been extremely helpful. Clark Potts, who designed the cover, and Alvin Jennings, the publisher, have given valuable assistance.

The Hillcrest elders have been a constant source of encouragement during the composition of this material.

The conclusions of the book are mine. I must bear the responsibility of any error. It is hoped that this material will prompt other men to examine this subject to point out the weaknesses or further strengthen the positions taken in this book.

Jimmy Jividen

February, 1971

DEDICATION

PREFACE

This book is a very thorough study of the roots, history, and fruit of the phenomenon of glossolalia, or "tongue-speaking". There have been resurgences of this practice throughout history. It is in no way limited either to the Christian religion or New Testament times. Heathen experience it. "Christian" cults steeped in the deepest die of religious error experience it. Some members of the Lord's church experience it.

None would seriously doubt the sincerity of those who claim such an experience, whether they be heathen, Jew, Catholic, or Protestant. Nor would anyone doubt that these people have experienced some sort of personal experience. The real question is whether this experience is the guidance of God's Spirit, as most claim, or whether it has its origin in completely different soil. Does it originate in the power of God and proceed out from Him to objectively influence certain people or does it originate in the people themselves and issue out in a subjective manifestation?

We know too little about the Holy Spirit. We have had no occasion to give really deep and scholarly study to the subject until recently. The many conflicting and erroneous views presented concerning the Spirit and His workings is evidence of how little we know. Many of the arguments we make in battling the claims of the glossolalia group will not hold water. When they see the weakness of our arguments, it is taken by them as evidence of their holding the truth in the matter. This isn't the case at all. It isn't a case of their having the truth; it is a case of our knowing too little about the subject to make sound arguments.

This book is written to remedy that situation. It is one of the most exhaustive treatments of the subject in print. Much new, and hither-to unpublished, material is here presented. There is a vast difference in the "tongues" of the New Testament and the glossolalia of today. It is clearly shown in this book that the "tongues" of the New Testament were languages, whereas the glossolalia of today is simply ecstatic gibberish. It does not make sense to think that God would take a man who can speak a language with intelligence and operate upon him in such a way as to leave him wholly incapable of speaking any language coherently. God does not destroy the rational and replace it with the irrational.

Restoration pioneers were quite familiar with "tongue-speaking", which was the natural substitution of experiementalism for God's revelation. All the religious denominations practiced it to a greater or lesser degree in direct ratio to their faith in the all-sufficiency of the Bible. As our pioneers struggled to hammer out a theology that incorporated faith in the all-sufficiency of the Scritpures as a sole rule of faith and practice, experimentalism gradually disappeared. Glossolalia is not a new thing; it was one of the ever-present problems of the early Restoration. We simply have to fight that battle all over again as the cycle of history gets back around to it again.

A treatment of the New Testament text in the orthodox tradition adds weight, as it always does, to the view that "tongue-speaking" has its roots in other than biblical ground.

In fact, glossolalia must be dealt with as a psychological problem, rather than a scriptural problem. It is a psychological problem. The logical and practical aspects of it are better understood by psychologists and counselors than by theologians and average church members.

The real issue involved in "tongue-speaking" is actually whether God exercises His authority through His word, or whether He exercises it directly by miracles, visions, present day revelations, modern apostles, and those to whom he gives special gifts. If the scriptures teach anything, they teach that revelation is complete in the Bible. It is hard for those suffering from glossolalia to understand why they are charged with discounting the authority and completeness of revelation. They have no desire to discredit God, and yet, the very claim of direct intervention cancels the contention for an all-sufficient Revelation. If either is true, the other is false. They cannot both be true. If God's Word is complete and perfect as a revelation, glossolalia is a psychological phenomenon and is to be dealt with as a psychological disorder, rather than a religious experience.

—Reuel Lemmons

TABLE OF CONTENTS

SECTION IV PSYCHOLOGICAL, LOGICAL AND PRACTICAL CONSIDERATIONS

INTRODUCTION

There is a new wave of the old practice of ecstatic utterances--commonly called "tongue speaking"--in religious circles. This phenomenon is not confined to minor religious sects. It has spread throughout both Protestantism and Catholicism. The experience has brought to some a revival of religious interest. It has touched the lives of individuals from nearly every educational, economic, and cultural background. Between two and three million adherents are claimed in the United States alone.

A prime educational force in the spread of this practice has been The Full Gospel Business Men Fellowship International--FGBMFI. This organization has grown from a small beginning in 1950 in Los Angeles, California to an international organization that could boast 6500 registrants at the 1970 convention. The primary thrust of this organization appears to be experiential religion with its accompanying practice of "speaking in tongues."

The practice of "tongue speaking" breaks through all denominational lines. Those who practice it seem to be concerned with a genuine spirit of ecumenism. Leaders of the movement strongly encourage their followers not to break with their present religious affiliation but remain in the group in order to lead others into this "spiritual revival."

This book is a reaction to the current "tongue speaking" phenomenon. The author seeks four things: (1) to understand what "tongue speaking" adherents are saying; (2) to compare the phenomenon with the New Testament gift of "speaking in tongues," and with similar phenomenon in psychology and world religions; (3) to show some of the theological consequences of accepting the doctrine; and (4) to suggest the kind of response the church should make to this movement.

This primary question is behind every chapter: Is the current phenomenon of "tongue speaking" from Heaven or from men? Is the practice merely ecstatic utterance brought about by a psychological release from within man or is it a supernatural gift of God to show divine approval? This question must be asked. It must be answered with as much objectivity as possible. No one can respond to the question without prior feelings about it. One will have prejudice which would lead him to identify the practice as being from man. Another will-- upon the basis of prior experiences--feel strongly that the practice is from God. Both prejudices and experiences are subjective and personal. The reader is encouraged to rise above both of these as he reads and examines the evidence in the light of Scripture and reason.

There are three presuppositions that are assumed by the author. First, Christ is the final and only religious authority.[1] Second, the Scriptures are the complete, final and only revelation of Jesus Christ and His teachings today.[2] Third, God has given man ability to think and reason. By this he is able to discern truth from error.[3] He is able to know the truth.[4]

Due to the subjective personal nature of "tongue speaking,"

1. Matthew 28:18.
2. II Timothy 3:15f.
3. I John 4:1.
4. John 8:32.

it is impossible to classify all who are involved in the practice in one category. The faith and practice of those who experience the "tongue speaking" phenomenon are often diverse and sometimes contradictory. The very nature of "tongue speaking" is highly individualistic and cannot be limited to any one faith. The author has attempted to discuss the phenomenon as he has found it most widely accepted. There is much disagreement concerning the nature, purpose and interpretation of glossolalia among the advocates of the practice. The author has tried to deal with underlying principles which would apply to almost all situations.

The author does not reject feeling in religion. Certainly a man who has been saved by the grace of God feels differently from a sin-laden person damned to hell. He rejoices just as the early Christians did after they were baptized into Christ.[5] When one is baptized into Christ, he is raised out of his baptism-burial to "walk in newness of life."[6] Surely he feels differently. When one leaves feeling out of Christianity--it is left cold and lifeless. It is dead. Just as the body without the spirit is dead, so religion without feeling is dead also. Neither should reason be left out of religion. When reason is ignored, all that is left is subjective emotionalism. There is confusion. There can be no objective standard to follow. Every man ends up doing what is right in his own eyes. Both the head and the heart are necessary in following Jesus. The heart gives reason motivation and spirit. The head gives the feelings of the heart logical direction and consistence.

The author does not deny that every person baptized after the New Testament pattern receives the gift of the Holy Spirit. The promise is clear.[7] Every child of God has the Spirit

5. Acts 2:38-47; 8:39.
6. Romans 6:4.
7. Acts 2:38; 5:32; I Corinthians 12:13.

of God dwelling in him.[8] The acceptance of the indwelling of the Holy Spirit and His work in the lives of Christians does not mean that one accepts the "tongue speaking" phenomenon as being from God.

The question is not whether God still works dynamically and wonderously in the lives of Christians by his Holy Spirit. Certainly he does. The queston is whether ecstatic utterances known as "tongue speaking" are a part of this work. The question is whether feelings and experience associated with "tongue speaking" are proof of divine sanction.

The following chapters will be posing these questions:

1. Is the present "tongue speaking" phenomenon a fulfillment of a New Testament promise, or is it religious error which is trying to be read back into the New Testament text?

2. Is the "tongue speaking" experience helpful to spirituality, or does it contain the seeds of destructive doubt?

3. Is the "tongue speaking" experience a sign of Christian maturity or evidence of spiritual babyhood?

4. Is the "tongue speaking" experience a divine sign or a delusion of the devil?

5. Is the "tongue speaking" experience a miracle or an explainable psychological phenomenon?

---

8. Romans 8:11; I Corinthians 6:19.

SECTION I

CHAPTER 1

GLOSSOLALIA

Descriptions of Glossolalia

The "tongue speaking" phenomenon today is often called glossolalia. This term first began to be used to describe the religious exercise of "tongue speaking" in the nineteenth century.[1] The term comes from the Greek word *glossa* which is translated "tongue" in the New Testament. Those who experience the present day phenomenon of "tongue speaking" identify it with the New Testament gift and therefore like to use a New Testament term to describe it.

Glossolalia is sometimes defined as "ecstatic speech often connected with religious excitement."[2] Ira J. Martin, in a doctoral dissertation at Boston Univeristy in 1942, describes it thus:

The nature of glossolalia is therefore frenzied, inarticular jargon with a sprinkling of coherent ejaculations whose inflections and tonal qualities have characteristics of speech.[3]

Certainly this description fits the phenomenon often found in Pentecostal meetings since 1900. This definition suggests that (1) it is not understood, (2) the speaker is in a frenzied state

1. W. G. H. Simon, The First Epistle to the Corinthians (London: SCM Press Ltd., 1959), p. 132.
2. R. R. Williams, The Acts of the Apostles (London: SCM Press Ltd., 1953), p. 42.
3. Ira J. Martin, Glossolalia in the Apostolic Church (An unpublished doctoral dissertation at Boston University, 1942), p. 48.

and (3) it has certain characteristics of speech.

Morton R. Kelsey, who has studied glossolalia with sympathy describes it thus:

> *It is a spontaneous utterance of uncomprehended and seemly random speech in sounds . . . . The speech itself rises in an effortless flow of unusually complex structure, with the repetition and inflection characteristic of language. It is neither controlled nor directly understood by the speaker, but takes possession of his speech. While occasionally a listener can identify a foreign language known to him, but not the speaker, the meaning is almost always spoken by an interpretation.*[4]

Three things may be noted in this definition: (1) The speech is spontaneous--not coming from the consciousness of the speaker. (2) The speech is not understood by the speaker, and except for phrases it is not understood by any of the listeners. (3) The speech has characteristics of language.

Geroge Barton Cutten, one time president of Colgate, describes the phenomenon from a psychological point of view, He says:

> *Whatever may be predicted of the psychological conditions of speaking with tongues in the New Testament, it is evident that the experience since then may be classed as ecstasy or allied phenomena. In ecstacy there is a condition of emotional exaltation, in which the one who experiences it is more or less oblivious of the external world, and loses to some extent his self-consciousness and his power of rational thought and self-control.*[5]

4. Morton T. Kelsey, Tongue Speaking (Doubleday and Co., Inc.: New York, 1964), p. 1.
5. George Barton Cutten, Speaking with Tongues (New Haven: Yale University Press, 1927), p. 157.

Cutten further observes that others suggest the conditions of catalepsy or hysteria instead of ecstacy. In this definition one finds that (1) the speech comes from the subconscious and (2) the speaker is in a state of emotional exaltation.

Stuart Bergsma also describes glossolalia as a psychological phenomenon. He writes that it is an:

Ecstasy, catalepsy, mass hysteria, a psychological state in which the consciously controlling apparatus of the mind is not dominant, a state in which the primitive reactions find their way to the surface, a state in which speech continues after thought is exhausted and a series of meaningless syllables results.[6]

In this definition one finds, (1) the speaker is in a state of emotional instability; (2) the unconscious part of the mind takes control; (3) the speech is meaningless syllables.

A summary definition of "tongue speaking" would include these points:

1. The speaker would be in a state of emotional exaltation.
2. The utterance would be spontaneous.
3. The speaker would not understand the utterance.
4. Listeners would not understand the utterance.
5. Yet the utterance would have characteristics of language.

This definition would fit similar phenomenon found in most world religions, both ancient and modern. It would also fit cases of Spiritualism and what has been called demon

6. Stuart Bergsma, Speaking with Tongues (New York: Parker Book House, 1965), p. 9.

possession. Such a definition also fits the state of certain abnormal psychological phenomenon.

Interpretations of Glossolalia

Glossolalia has been interpreted as divine help for missionaries in communicating to those of a different language. Cutten documents cases of missionaries being sent out by Pentecostal groups who expected God to give them the gifts of tongues when they arrived on the mission field.[7] After several costly and disappointing attempts, this practice was discontinued. "Tongue speaking" has been associated with Mormonism since its beginning. Early Mormons often thought that the gift of tongues would aid them in the conversion of the Indians. Fawn Brodie tells of such a case when the Mormons were making a journey from Kirkland, Ohio, to Independence, Missouri: "At the beginning of the journey they

At the beginning of the journey they were buoyed up by extravagant hopes, some predicting mass conversions of of the Indians through the gift of tongues. . . . . . . "[8]

Although one still hears of claims of missionaries obtaining the gift of tongues to aid them in their work, it is always vague references in far off places.

Glossolalia is sometimes interpreted as languages known in previous existences. Spiritualists take this view. William James relates a case of a Spiritualist who spoke in a language that he thought he had known in a previous existence. The Spiritualist could not identify the language, but assumed that this was the source.[9] Cutten documents a case of a French woman who

7. Geroge Barton Cutten, op. cit., pp. 124-25.
8. Fawn M. Brodie, *No Man Knows My History* (New York: A. A. Knopf, 1945), p. 114.
9. Proceedings of the Society of Psychical Research, Vol. XII, p. 277f.

claimed to have had a former existence as the wife of a Hindoo prince and could thus speak that language.[10] This same woman in a trance often spoke in what she called the language of the people who lived on Mars. The claims of the Spiritualists are the same as those who claim the glossolalia experience in the name of Jesus Christ. The evidence of one is as weighty as the evidence of the other. How can one be from God and the other from the devil?

Glossolalia has traditionally been interpreted as demon possession in Roman Catholicism. Among the signs which the Roman Catholic Church uses for determining demon possession are:

> *Use or knowledge of an unknown language; knowledge of distant or hidden facts; manifestation of physical force beyond the age or condition of the subject.* [11]

The belief that speaking in tongues indicates demon possession is not limited to Roman Catholicism. Cutten relates a case of a boy thought to be possessed by a demon as told by a cultured Brahmin in India:

> *. . . (This man's son) . . . suffered from strange spells which increased in frequency. During these seizures he seemed normal except somewhat more sensitive, nervous, and suspicious, and he would speak in a strange voice or in different voices, and when using one voice his speech was a wild gibberish.* [12]

One should not be too quick to reject this explanation of glossolalia. The Scriptures teach that the devil still is active. As a roaring lion, he walks about seeking whom he may devour.[13]

10. Cutten, op. cit., p. 136f.

11. Bernard Martin, Healing for You (Richmond: John Knox Press, 1965), p. 103.

12. Cutten, op. cit., p. 105.

13. I Peter 5:8

He is able to fashion himself into an angel of light.[14] The devil and his unholy spirits would certainly try to deceive the world by trying to duplicate the work of the Holy Spirit. There is a lot that the Scriptures do not say about demons and the spiritual hosts of Satan. One must not discount the possibility that glossolalia might be a delusion of the devil. There is a spirit that works in the sons of disobedience. [15]

Glossolalia is often interpreted on purely psychological grounds. Credibility is given to this interpretation by examples of similar phenomenon completely outside the religious context. F. W. H. Myers gives good documentation of this from the works of Pierre Janet and Sigmund Freud.[16]

Janet relates a case of Maria who talked and wrote automatically without conscious effort. Maria reported:

When I want to sing it is impossible to me; yet at other times I hear my voice sing the song very well. It is certainly not I who walks; I feel like a balloon which jumps up and down of itself. When I want to write I find nothing to say, my head is empty, and I must let my hand write what it chooses, and it fills four pages, and if the stuff is silly I cannot help it.[17]

Freud relates the case of Fraulein Anna O. who after great emotional stress developed a cleavage in her personality.[18] There was a split between her conscious thought and her actions

---

14. II Corinthians 11:14.
15. Ephesians 2:2.
16. F. W. H. Myers, Human Personality and Its Survival of Bodily Death (New Hyde Park: University Book Co., 1961), pp. 30-42.
17. Pierre Janet, L'Etat Mental des Hysteriques (Paris, 1893).
18. Sigmund Freud, Studeis uber Hysterie (Leipsig, 1895).

coming from her unconsciousness. Myers relates the case:

> *Disturbances of speech may give very delicate indications*
> *of internal turmoil of the personality; and Fraulein O's*
> *great linguistic gift made her perhaps the most interesting*
> *example on record of hysterical aphasia and paraphasia.*
> *Sometimes she was altogether speechless. Sometimes she*
> *talked German in ungrammatical fashion.   Sometimes*
> *she spoke English, apparently believing it to be German,*
> *but understood German; sometimes she spoke English*
> *and could not understand German.*[19]

These examples related by Myers show that in certain cases of
disintegration of the personality, automatic speech is produced
similar to its religious counterpart glossolalia.

This interpretation is also shared by Cutten in his psychological studies of speaking in tongues. He writes:

> *In considering speaking with tongues we have to do with*
> *a state of personal disintegration, which the vorbo-*
> *motive centers of the subject are obedient to subcon-*
> *scious impulses.*[20]

The psychological description of glossolalia helps one to
understand it. It is one thing to show that it is an explainable
phenomenon in abnormal psychology. It is another thing to
say that neither the Holy Spirit nor the demonic spirits of the
devil have anything to do with it. If it can be shown that the
glossolalia experience is not Biblical and contrary to the workings of the Holy Spirit in our time, it will become evident that
it is either from the devil or the product of man's own psyche.

---

19. Myers, op. cit., p. 42.
20. Cutten, op. cit., p. 160
21. Raphael Gasson, **The Challenging Counterfeit** (Plainfield, New
Jersey: Logos Books, 1970). Gasson advocates that glossolalia practiced in Spiritualism a counterfeit from the Devil while that practiced
by Neo-Pentecostals is real and from God.

Glossolalia is often interpreted by its advocates today as a private devotional exercise, and only to be used in public when interpreted.[22]

This interpretation makes it easier for its advocates to conform the present practice to the regulations set down by Paul in I Corinthians 14. Paul said:

> *Howbeit in the church I had rather speak five words with my understanding, that I might instruct others also, than ten thousand words in a tongue.*

> *When you come together, each one hath a psalm, hath a teaching, hath a revelation, hath a tongue, hath an interpretation, let all things be done unto edifying.*[23]

These passages would prohibit any speech in the assembly which could not be understood by the hearers. This would apply to the New Testament gift of language as well as the present practice of ecstatic utterances.

This interpretation also keeps down opposition from religious bodies which do not generally practice glossolalia. If one insists that his use of glossolalia is only for his private devotion, it appears quite innocent. Many religious leaders would view this as only an insignificant matter of opinion and tolerate it.

What Kind of Language?

Those who practice glossolalia differ on the exact nature of the speech. It is believed to be from God, but what language is it, if it be a language?

22. Howard M. Ervin, "As the Spirit Gives Utterance," *Christianity Today* (April 11, 1969), p. 624.
23. I Corinthians 14:19, 26.

As has already been suggested, some have believed that glossolalia was a divine gift to help missionaries communicate with those of other nations.[24] This theory was widely held at one time, but came into disfavor when it did not work on the mission field.

I Corinthians 13 speaks of the "tongues of angels.[25] Using this passage as a starting point some have suggested that glossolalia is a heavenly language spoken by angels. Maurice Barnett writes: *"The language of heaven is unintelligible and unspeakable to ordinary men. Only enlightened men may be fit to hear and reproduce it."* [26] Such a statement goes beyond wnat is said in the onetime reference to the "tongues of angels." Such an interpretation is based upon a very materialistic view of heaven and spiritual beings. The New Testament teaches that angels are spirits.[27] There is no indication that they have some special language in which to communicate with one another. If such a language existed, it certainly would not be like sounds coming from flesh and blood organs of speech.[28]

Genesis 11 contains a story of the tower of Babel. Moses said before God's judgment on the people building the tower that: *"The whole earth was of one language, and of one speech."*[29] Some suggest that glossolalia is the true language of Adam spoken before the confusion of tongues at the tower of Babel. In their view Pentecost was the reversal of Babel. B. H. Carroll writes:

24. See Page 46ff.
25. See page 116f.
26. Maurice Barnett, The Living Flame (London: The Epworth Press, 1953), p. 28.
27. Hebrews 1:14.
28. See page 116f.
29. Genesis 11:1.

> *The object of the coming of the Holy Spirit in Acts 2*
> *was in part to restore the unity of the long-severed frag-*
> *ments of the human race into one family of God. The*
> *gift of tongues is to indicate how this unity is to be*
> *brought about.*[30]

This theory does not have objective evidence to support it. On Pentecost men did not hear in one common Adamic language-- but in the language wherein he was born.[31] Both history and experience demonstrate that a common Adamic language did not exist after Pentecost. There is still a confusion of languages in the world.

Some advocates of glossolalia interpret their speech as being primitive languages. This certainly removes the possibility of a critical comparison of glossolalia with any known language of the world. Who could compare the recorded speech of one "speaking in tongues" today with the language of cultures long dead? There is no way to either prove or disprove that glosso- lalia is a primitive language. There is no objective criteria with which to examine it.

A more common interpretation of the nature of glossolalia is that it is a spiritual language given by the Holy Spirit to ex- press the deepest emotions of men which cannot be expressed in regular language. H. L. Goudge write:

> *Lanaguage at its best lags behind thought, and fails to*
> *express our deepest emotions. . . . May we not then be-*
> *lieve that, at its highest, the language of the tongues was*
> *a language which the Spirit created, the Spirit's answer to*

30. B. H. Carroll, The Acts (Nashville: The Broadman Press, 1942), p. 34.
31. Acts 2:8.

the need that the Spirit had created.[32]

This interpretation does not fit the New Testament gift of tongues. The New Testament gift was languages which men spoke.[33]

Some who practice glossolalia recognize that externally it is a psychological phenomenon common to both world religions and abnormal psychology. Even though the external evidence is the same, they would insist that their experience comes from God even though others can be psychologically explained. A letter to the editor in the Journal of American Scientific Affiliation expresses this view. Paul Seely writes:

> *The statement, "that bizarre utterances occur in non-Christian cultures emphasizes the fact the practice is not self-authenticating" is misleading. The practice is not self-authenticating so far as its externals are concerned: but to the participant, the Holy Spirit bears a witness that is as self-authenticating as one's consciousness of existence.*[34]

Such a view places the subject completely in the realm of subjectivism. It is a resurgence of the old doctrine of "it's true, because I feel it down in my heart--no matter what external facts point to the contrary."

Perhaps glossolalia is able to gain followers in so many religious groups today because there has been a neglect of validating religious truth by the objective standard of the Scriptures. The "inward testimony of the Holy Spirit" has long

32. H. L. Goudge, The First Epistle to the Corinthians (Westminister Commentaries, ed. Walter Lock. (London: Methuen and Co., 1911), p. 136.

33. See page 35ff.

34. Paul H. Seely, "Letters to the Editor," Journal of the American Scientific Affiliation, Vol. XX, NO. 3, (September, 1968), p. 93.

been a criteria for determining religious truths among most "fundamentalists" groups.[35] It is no wonder that those who have accepted such a doctrine would also accept the possibility of the "inward workings of the Holy Spirit" in glossolalia.

The different theories advanced by advocates of glossolalia show that there is much disagreement among them. It is difficult to understand how a gift claiming to come from God could have so many conflicting interpretations among its recipients. God is not a God of confusion!

A description of the phenomenon as understood by the author would be:

Glossolalia is a psychological phenomenon found in most world religions, both ancient and modern, and often completely outside of religious context. It has no rational meaning but consists of mere ecstatic utterances.

35. Edward J. Young, An Introduction to the Old Testament (Grand Rapids: Wm. B. Eerdmans Publishing Co., 1949), p. 38.

CHAPTER 2

THE MEANING OF "TONGUES" IN THE NEW TESTAMENT

The gift of tongues is mentioned in the seven chapters in the New Testament.[1] One time it is a promise of Jesus. Three times it is used by Luke as he recorded events in the early church. Three times it is used by Paul in writing to the church at Corinth concerning their abuse of the gift.

Glossa

Glossa is the Greek word that is translated "tongue" in the New Testament. The word was not confined to merely the "gift of tongues" but was also used in other ways.

Liddell-Scott gives three general uses of *glossa* in Attic Greek.[2] (1) The tongue, as a member of the body--an organ of speech.[3] (2) It means a language or dialect--referring to foreign or obsolete words which needed translation or explanation.[4] (3) It means "anything shaped like a tongue"--like the tongue

---

1. Mark 16:17; Acts 2, 10, 19; I Corinthians 12, 13, 14.
2. George H. Liddell and Robert Scott, A Greek-English Lexison of New Testament Greek (New York: Charles Scribner's Sons, 1895), p. 312.
3. James 3:5.
4. Acts 2:6.

of a shoe or a tongue of land jutting out into the sea.[5]

Behm's article on *Glossa* in Kittel's Theological Dictionary of the New Testament documents a number of references outside the New Testament in which *glossa* is used to refer to ecstatic utterances in pagan cults. Glossolalia or ecstatic utterances were known in New Testament times in the enthusiastic cults like the Thracian Dionysus cult, the Delphic of Phrygia and the Sybils. An impressive list of examples of erratic speech is given by Behn to show that ecstatic utterances were quite common in New Testament times as well as throughout Greek history. After giving these examples from pagan cults, Behm draws the conclusion that the same thing was going on in the church at Corinth. He writes:

In Corinth, therefore, glossolalia is an unintelligible ecstatic utterance. One of its forms of expression is a muttering of words or sounds without interconnection or meaning. Parallels may be found for this phenomenon in various forms and at various places in religious history.[6]

It is true that such ecstatic utterances were practiced in the pagan cults in New Testament times. *Glossa* is one of the Greek terms that was used with reference to these ecstatic utterances. This does not necessarily mean, however, that the "gift of tongues" in the New Testament was the same thing. These points should be considered. (1) Nothing in the New Testament would suggest that its use of *glossa* referred to ecstatic utterances.[7] The "tongues"--*glossa*--on Pentecost are clearly

5. Acts 2:3.

6. Johannes Behm, "Glossa," Theological Dictionary of the New Testament edited by Gerhard Kittel, Vol. I. (Grand Rapids, Wm. E. Eerdmans, 1964), p. 722.

7. It will later be shown that there is a possibility that pagans were coming into the Corinthians assembly giving ecstatic utterances. Since the Corinthians were abusing the real gift of tongues–languages– these pagans could go undetected and pronounce "Jesus is anathema." See page 111ff.

identified as language[8] and there is no hint in the other passages that the meaning had changed. (2) If the New Testament "tongues"--*glossa*--were the same as the ecstatic utterance of the pagan cults, the super-natural nature of the gift would be denied. There would be nothing miraculous in the apostles doing the same thing that all the pagan cults were doing. The New Testament gift of tongues was to be a sign to follow the preaching of the gospel. It showed that the message was from God.[9] The sign would not have meaning if it were no more than experiences common in the pagan cults. (3) In defining a word in the New Testament, it must first be considered in light of its use in the New Testament itself. For example, the Greek word, *logos* translated "Word" in the Gospel of John means an impersonal force governing the world in the Greek Stoic writings. In John it refers to the eternal personal God who became flesh.[10]

Thayer recognized a poetical and rhetorical usage of *glossa* in the New Testament.[11] This usage ascribes to a member of the body that which belongs to the whole man. *"Therefore did my heart rejoice, and my tongue was glad,"*[12] and, *"With their tongues they have used deceit,"*[13] are examples of such a use.

From the foregoing, four New Testament meanings can be given to *glossa*. (1) A physical organ in the mouth; (2) language or dialect; (3) anything that looks like a tongue; (4) poetic and rhetorical usage.

Another use of *glossa* is to be found in Greek literature

8 Acts 2:6, 8, 11.
9 Mark 16:17-20.
10 John 1:1-4,14.
11 Joseph Henry Thayer, A Greek-English Lexicon (New York: American Book Co., 1889), p. 118.
12 Acts 2:26.
13 Romans 3:13

outside the New Testament. This usage is "ecstatic utterance" found in the enthusiastic pagan cults. It is a distinctive mark of early Christianity that such irrational practice found no part in its worship.

Glossa in English
Translations

A part of the confusion of understanding the nature of "tongues" in the New Testament comes from different translations. Translations sometimes follow the Greek pagan concept of *glossa* which referred to ecstatic utterance when used in a religious context. They have brought the same meaning into the New Testament text.

The translators of the King James Version (KJV) added "unknown" before "tongue" in I Corinthians 14:2: *"For he that speaketh in an unknown tongue speaketh not unto men, but unto God."* It is in italics showing that it was added by the translators. There is no word for *"unknown"* in the Greek text. It was added by the translator in an effort to clarify the meaning. To some it did just the opposite. These understood "unknown tongues" to be a heavenly language known only to God.[14]

Today's English Version (TEV) adds to the translation confusion. In Jesus' statement in the Gospel of Mark, it reads: *"Believers will be given these signs of power: they will drive out demons in my name; they will speak in strange tongues . . . ."*[15] In the account of the baptism of the Holy Spirit on

14. This is not to suggest that adding a word to the text is poor translation. It is often necessary to convey the full meaning of the original. It is the judgment of this author as well as the translators of other English versions that such is not warranted in this case.

15. Mark 16:17.

the day of Pentecost, *glossa* is translated two ways in the same context. The text reads:

> *Then they saw what looked like tongues of fire spreading out; and each person there was touched by a tongue. They were all filled with the Holy Spirit and began to talk in other languages, as the Spirit enabled them to speak.*[16]

Both "tongues" and "languages" are translated from the Greek *glossa*. Adding even more confusion, *glossa* is translated as "strange sounds" in I Corinthians.

> *To one man he gives the ability to speak with strange sounds; to another, he gives the ability to explain what these sounds mean.*
>
> *The one who speaks with strange sounds does not speak to men but to God, because no one understands him.* [17]

Glossa is translated "strange sounds" in Acts 10:46 and 19:6. According to Robert Gundry such a translation is not justified.[18]

Between chapters 12 and 14 of I Corinthians, *glossa* is again translated "languages". "I may be able to speak the *languages* of men and even of angels."[19] In the same context of I Corinthians 13 *glossa* is translated "gifts of speaking." The TEV translation of I Corinthians 13:8 is *"Love is eternal. There are inspired messages, but they are temporary; there are gifts of speaking, but they will cease."*

The English reader would have difficulty knowing that

16. Acts 2:3-4.
17. I Corinthians 12:10, 14:2
18. Robert, H. Gundry, " 'Ecstatic Utterance' (N. E. B.)?" The Journal of Theological Studies XVII (October, 1966), pp. 299-307.
19. I Corinthians 13:1.

all of these words are translations of the same Greek word. The translation is "tongues" in Mark 16. *Glossa* is translated "tongues" and "languages" in the same context of Acts 2. The translation is "strange sounds" in Acts 10:46; 19:6 and in I Corinthians 12-14. In I Corinthians 13 *glossa* is translated both "gifts of speaking" and "languages" In the Greek text, the same word is used in each case.

It is the context which determines how the word is to be translated. As already shown *glossa* can be translated four ways. In Acts 2:3 it is evident from the context that "tongues of fire" must be understood rather than "languages of fire." *"Glossa"* in the other passages noted refers to speech of men. There is nothing in the context which would indicate that this speech should be translated "tongues" in Mark, "languages" in Acts 2, "strange sounds" in Acts 10:46, 19:6 and in I Corinthians 12-14, and gifts of speaking" in I Corinthians 13:8. The word is the same. The contexts of the different passages do not demand such a variety of translations. In the TEV it would appear that at least four different phenomena were meant. No wonder there is confusion.

The New English Bible (NEB) also lacks consistency in translating *glossa* in these passages. It imposes an erroneous interpretation into the text by translating it "language of ecstasy." In Mark, Acts 2, and I Corinthians 13, *glossa* is translated "tongues." In Acts 10:46 and 19:6 it is translated "tongues of ecstasy." In I Corinthians 12 and 14 the translation is "language of ecstasy." The translation of I Corinthians 14:2 reads: *"When a man is using the language of ecstasy, he is talking with God, not with men, for no man understands him."* The use of "tongues of ecstasy" and "languages of ecstasy" is clearly an unwarranted translation. The Greek has a word for ecstasy. It was *ekstasis.* This word is not used in the whole context. In fact it is never used in the New Testament in connection with *glossa*.

Certainly the work of translation is difficult. It is the translators' task not only to translate to the nearest word, but also to the nearest thought. The context must determine the translation. There is nothing in either the word *glossa* or the context in which it is used for such a variety of translations. Sometimes theological bias hinders good translation. Perhaps this is the case in these passages. The translators of the KJV, TEV and NEB have added to the misunderstanding of "tongues" in the New Testament. The ASV and the RSV are at least consistent in their translation of *glossa*. They always use "tongues."

Meaning of Glossa in the

New Testament

It is important to study the use of a New Testament word by seeing how it is used in the broad spectrum of Greek literature. It is also important to see how the word has been translated in different versions. The ultimate test, however, must come from an examination of the word in the text of the New Testament itself. How is *glossa* to be understood in its New Testament usage?

In the New Testament *glossa* is the term used to describe one of the gifts which was received through the Holy Spirit. The gift of "tongues" *glossa* is found connected with the baptism of the Holy Spirit,[20] and with the gifts received through

20. Acts 2:1-4; 10:44-47.

the laying on of the apostles' hands.[21] Each time the New Testament speaks of individuals receiving the gift of "tongues" it is connected with the Holy Spirit.[22] The New Testament evidence points to the fact that the *glossa* gift, along with other miraculous gifts, could only be received by the baptism of the Holy Spirit or the laying on of the apostles' hands.[23]

In the New Testament, the *glossa* gift was considered an inferior gift. It is listed with the other miraculous gifts of prophecies and knowledge as being inferior to the abiding non-miraculous gifts of faith, hope, and love.[24] Even among the miraculous gifts, the *glossa* gift was considered inferior to prophesying. Paul says:

> *Now I would have you all speak with tongues, but rather that ye should prophesy: for greater is he that prophesieth than he that speaketh with tongues . . . . Howbeit in the church I had rather speak five words with my understanding, that I might instruct others also, than ten thousand words in a tongue.*[25]

As a gift inferior to prophesying, *glossa* was tightly regulated by Paul. It was not to be used in the church unless there was an interpreter present.[26] Not more than two or three individuals were to use the gift of tongues at one time. Even then it was to be in turn.[27]

As a gift inferior to faith, hope, and love, *glossa* was to pass away with the other temporary gifts.[28] The need of these

21. Acts 19:6.
22. See also I Corinthians 12:4-10.
23. See page 145ff.
24. I Corinthians 13:8-13.
25. I Corinthians 14:5a, 19.
26. I Corinthians 14:28.
27. I Corinthinas 14:27.
28. I Corinthians 13:8.

miraculous, temporary gifts was to cease and hence the gifts
would cease.[29]

The contents of the *glossa* gift is described in different ways
in the New Testament. On the day of Pentecost the content of
the gift was "speaking . . . the mighty words of God."[30] At
the household of Cornelius the content of the gift was speaking
to "magnify God."[31] Paul suggests that the content of the
gift was "mysteries" when there was no one present who un-
stood.[32] He also suggests that even though the contents of
these spiritual utterances of *glossa* were that of "blessing" or
"giving of thanks," it would be unprofitable to those who did
not understand.[33] From these passages it is clear that
the contents of the *glossa* gift was praise, teaching, blessing
and giving thanks. When it was not understood by others
present, it was to them "mysteries" and not profitable.

The use of the *glossa* gift in the early church was for edifying the church. To use the gift without interpretation was
without profit.[34] A listener would be unable to say "amen"
at the giving of thanks, if he did not understand what was being said.[35] Pagan visitors coming into the assembly of the
church would think the Christians were mad if they used the
glossa gift without interpretation.[36] Paul gives very clear instructions about the use of this unusual gift: *"When ye come
together, each one hath a psalm, hath a teaching, hath an*

29. See page 144f.
30. Acts 2:11.
31. Acts 10:46.
32. I Corinthians 14:2.
33. I Corinthians 14:16-17.
34. I Corinthians 14:6.
35. I Corinthians 14:16.
36. I Corinthians 14:23-25.

interpretation. Let all things be done unto edifying.''[37]

The very nature of the *glossa* gift made it inferior to prophecy. If God were giving an inspired message to the church
at Corinth, he could do it either through one person prophesying or through two persons speaking in tongues and interpreting. The latter was the long way of doing it. Why use two
when one would do? Some at Corinth were using the *glossa*
gift in pride. It was a showy gift and the possessors thought it
made them among the spiritual elite. I Corinthians 12-14 was
written by Paul to correct those who were abusing the *glossa*
gift. They needed to learn that the *glossa* gift did not make
them better than other Christians. Neither did it make them
spiritually mature.

Chapter 12 shows that the same spirit was the source of all
of the gifts and each gift was to be used for the good of all.[38]
Being the possessor of a showy gift did not make that member
more important or more needed than other members of the
body of Christ.[39]

Chapter 13 shows that the *glossa* gift without love makes one
like sounding brass or a clanging symbal.[40] The gift was showy
and noisy, but worthless unless the possessor had love. This
chapter also shows that the *glossa* gift was only temporary
and would pass away.[41] The Christians at Corinth were encouraged to possess faith, hope and love more than temporary
passing gifts.[42]

Chapter 14 shows that the *glossa* gift was inferior to

37. I Corinthians 14:25.
38. I Corinthians 12:7.
39. I Corinthians 12:21-22.
40. I Corinthians 13:1.
41. I Corinthians 13:8.
42. I Corinthians 12:31.

prophecy.[43]   Its abuse by its proud possessors had been a point of confusion in the church at Corinth.[44]   Tight regulations were given for its use.

The *glossa* gift in the early church must be understood as languages. All of the New Testament evidence points toward this. It was identified as languages known by men when it first came upon the apostles on the day of Pentecost. All of the other evidence in the New Testament fits this early definition. There is no need to try to read the pagan phenomenon of ecstatic utterance back into the New Testament text. If the *glossa* gift could be explained psychologically as the pagan phenomenon the miraculous element would be gone. In interpreting the Scriptures, one should always interpret the unknown in terms of the known. It is known that the *glossa* gift was languages on Pentecost.[45] It should be so interpreted in other places unless inspired men redefine it.

43. I Corinthians 14:5.
44. I Corinthians 14:33.
45. Acts 2:6, 8, 11.

CHAPTER 3

ECSTATIC UTTERANCES OR LANGUAGES

Much of the confusion that exists over "tongue speaking" is over the misunderstanding of the nature of the *glossa* gift in the New Testament. Four different views are generally held today concerning the nature of the New Testament gift.

(1) Ability to speak in a foreign language without having learned it.[1]

(2) Ecstatic utterances coming from a supernatural working of the Holy Spirit.

(3) A combination of the above views which makes the gift on the day of Pentecost foreign languages and the phenomenon in the church at Corinth ecstatic utterances.[2]

(4) Ecstatic utterances which are nothing more than psychological phenomenon explainable in human terms.[3]

In studying the New Testament evidence, one must be careful not to interpret the New Testament phenomenon in terms of the glossolalia experience today. They are to be studied independently. Only after one has discovered the nature of the *glossa* gift in the New Testament can he compare it to the

1. Howard M. Ervin. "As the Spirit Gives Utterance," Christianity Today, (April 11, 1969), p. 623f.
2. Carl G. Tuland. "The Confusion About Tongues," Christianity Today. (December 6, 1968), p. 207f.
3. This view is generally held by those who deny the supernatural signs of the New Testament.

present phenomenon.

Jesus predicted "tongue speaking." After he gave the great commission in Mark, He says: *"And these signs shall accompany them that believe: in my name shall they cast out demons; they shall speak with new tongues . . . ."*[4] This promise was fulfilled on the day of Pentecost in Jerusalem; sometime later at the household of Cornelius in Caesarea; still later at Ephesus; and finally after many years at Corinth. The promise of Jesus was one. Its fulfillment must also be one. All of the occurrences of the fulfillment of the promise must be considered as one even though they are separated in time and distance. There is no evidence that any one fulfillment was different from the others.

The Definition of Luke

The first occurrence of "tongue speaking" in the New Testament was on the day of Pentecost. Luke gives a very full description of the phenomenon:

> *And they were all filled with the Holy Spirit, and began to speak with other tongues as the Spirit gave them utterance . . . the multitude came together, and were confounded, because that every man heard them speaking in his own language. And they were all amazed and marvelled, saying, Behold, are not all these that speak Galilaeans. And how hear we, every man in our own language where we were born; . . . . We hear them speaking in our tongues the mighty works of God.*[5]

Luke understood the gift to be languages. Three conclusive points show this in the account.

4. Mark 16:17.
5. Acts 2:4-8, 11.

First, Luke uses the words *glossa* and *dialektos* interchangeably. The apostles were speaking in tongues, *glossa*. The apostles were speaking in language, *dialektos*.[6] The tongues—or languages—that they spoke were not some heavenly unknown language. The languages were known by the men who heard. What they heard was their own native tongue—the langauge wherein they were born.

Second, the crowd that gathered around the apostles were amazed and marvelled. The men they saw were Galilaeans, but the language they heard was their own. The marvel of it all was that men who were known to be of one dialect could fluently speak another language.

Third, some fifteen nationalities are listed by Luke in connection with the "tongue speaking" sign. These nationalities probably refer to Jews of the dispersion who no longer knew Aramaic. If languages of these nationalities were not meant, why would these different nationalities be mentioned? The different nationalities were saying, "We hear them speaking in our tongues."

Pentecost was the first occurrence of the *glossa* gift and should thus be used to define the gift in other passages. The first time a thing is mentioned, it should be defined and described. Luke did this in Acts 2 and assumed that the reader understood the gift in the other passages.

It should also be noted that Luke was writing to Theophilus, *"that thou mightest know the certainty concerning the things wherein thou wast instructed."*[7] He must have been an unbeliever or a new convert who needed further instruction. It was necessary to explain the *glossa* gift to him. These to whom

6. Acts 2:4-6.
7. Luke 1:4.

Paul was writing in Corinth would not need such a definition. The *glossa* gift was very common there and had been known for a long time. Paul could assume that his reader would not need a definition, Luke could not. It would be foolish to ignore Luke's plain definition and try to pick a definition out of Paul's Corinthian letter. Frank Balch makes this same point.

> *Luke's description in Acts is decisive for what Paul writes to Corinth. Some scholars tend to reverse this process. They try to determine what happened at Corinth and then to either square the two accounts or conclude that two different gifts are mentioned . . . . Luke is the one who fully describes what the tongues are, while Paul takes for granted that his readers know what they are and therefore offers no description . . . . Luke writes for a reader (Theophilus) who may not have heard of the gift. Paul writes for readers who have often heard members of their own congregation speak in tongues.*[8]

If a word is used to describe a practice in the New Testament, it should always be taken to mean the same thing in other places unless the new context will not allow it.

The Phenomenon at Corinth

Paul did not need to define the *glossa* gift when he wrote to Corinth. Everyone understood it. Everything in the discussion of the gift in I Corinthians 12-14 fits the definition as given by Luke in Acts 2.

The use of *barbaros* in 14:11 would indicate that the Corinthians understood the gift to be languages: *"If then I know not the meaning of the voice, I shall be to him that speaketh a*

8. Frank Balch. "I Corinthians 13" (Unpublished paper presented to Pepperdine College in 1956).

barbarian and he that speaketh will be a barbarian unto me.[9]
A barbarian in the Greek world was one who was not Greek in
culture and language. One of the major definitions of *barbaros*
given by Hans Windisch in the Theological Dictionary of the
New Testament is: " 'of a strange speech,' or 'the one who
speaks a strange language' (i.e., other than Greek.)"[10] The use
of *diermenouo* in I Corinthians 12:30, 14:5, 13, 27, would
allow languages to be understood as the gift of tongues in Corinth. Most versions translated *diermenouo* "interpret." The
verb can mean either "to translate" or "to interpret." The first
meaning given by the Arndt-Gingrich Lexicon is "to translate."
Johnnes Behn in the Theological Dictionary of the New Testament gives one meaning of the verb as being "to transfer from
a foreign language into familiar."[11] Some have tried to
make a case for the gift of tongues in Corinth being ecstatic
utterance by forcing *diermenouo* to mean only "to interpret"
and not "to translate." Carl Tuland affirms:

> *The tongue speaking in Corinth was ecstatic utterance
> or babbling, to be understood by others it had to be
> interpreted, but not translated.*"[12]

This can not be done. *Diermenouo* can not be confined in definition to just "to interpret." It also means "to
translate." The context determines which meaning is given to
it. To argue that the *glossa* gift was ecstatic utterance in Corinth and attempt to prove it by the definition of *diermenouo*
is uncritical. It assumes what is to be proven. It is circular
reasoning.

If the use of the context is to determine the meaning of the

9. I Corinthians 14:11.

10. Hans Windisch. ' Barbaros," Theological Dictionary of the New
Testament, edited by Gerhard Kittel, Vol. I, (Grand Rapids, Wm. B.
Eerdmans Publishing Co., 1964), pp. 546-47.

11. Johannes Behn. "Ermenueo," Theological Dictionary of the New
Testament, edited by Gerhard Kittel, Vol. II, (Grand Rapids, Wm. B. Eerdmans Publishing Co., 1964), pp. 762-63.

12. Carl G. Tuland, op. cit., p. 208.

verb, then "translate" would be the best term to use. Luke defines the *glossa* gift as languages in Acts 2. It must be assumed to have the same meaning throughout the New Testament unless a different context demands a different meaning. If *diermenouo* is to be translated by "to translate" and *glossa* is to be translated by "language," the meaning of I Corinthians 14:27-28 becomes more understandable.

> *If any man speaks in a language, let it be by two, or at the most three, and that in turn; and let one translate; but if there be no translator, let him keep silent in the church.*

Paul's quotation from Isaiah 28:11-12 within the discussion of the *glossa* gift shows that languages are meant.[13] It is clear from the context of Isaiah 28 that "other tongues"refers to the speech of foreigners. Isaiah rebukes the priests and prophets of Jerusalem because they rejected his message. He warns them that if they refuse to listen to his speech they will be forced to listen to the same message from the unaccustomed speech of foreign soldiers in their streets. He says: *"Nay, but by men of strange lips and with another tongue will he speak to this people . . . yet will they not hear."*[14] Isaiah was not speaking of ecstatic utterances, but of a foreign language. The apostle uses the context of the Isaiah passage to teach a lesson to the Corinthians. Just as the priests and prophets of Isaiah's day refused the clear prophecy of Isaiah, the Corinthians did not care for the gift of prophecy. Just as those who rejected prophecy in Isaiah's day had to hear another language, the same was true members of the church at Corinth.[15]

13. I Corinthians 14:21.
14. Isaiah 28:11-12.
15. Jimmy Jividen, "Tongues Are for a Sign," Mission (July, 1969), pp. 15-17.

Some of the arguments in favor of interpreting *glossa* as ecstatic utterance in I Corinthians are thought to be found in the text itself. A collection of these arguments from several sources are as follows:

(1)   The speech is addressed to God (vss. 2, 28.)
(2)   The speaker in the spirit speaks mysteries (vs. 2.)
(3)   The speaker edifies himself and not others (vs. 4.)
(4)   The speaker's understanding is unfruitful (vs. 14.)
(5)   The speech was not understood by the hearers (vs. 19.)
(6)   Outsiders hearing the speech will think it is madness (vs. 23.)

It is true that all of these arguments fit ecstatic utterance. They also fit speaking in a foreign language that is not understood.

One with the gift of language would be speaking to God if neither he nor his hearers understood the language.

One with the gift of language would be speaking in the spirit since he had not learned the language by natural means. What he would be saying would be both a mystery to himself and his hearers who did not understand the language.

One with the gift of language would only be edifying himself with his speech if there were no one present who knew the language. No one else would understand his message and therefore could not be edified. He would not understand the message either but would be edified by the knowledge that God was using him to speak a foreign language.

One with the gift of language would not be understood by the hearers unless the language was known by them as was the case on Pentecost. The situation on the day of Pentecost was the only time in the New Testament accounts that there was a multilanguaged group assembled when the gift of tongues was exercised. In Ceasarea, Ephesus and Corinth one finds the gift being exercised. There is nothing said about understanding the speech except at Corinth and then only with the aid of an interpreter.

One with the gift of language speaking in an assembly in which no one understood would be acting irrationally. An outsider seeing this situation would think that it was madness.

Every argument that is used to identify the Corinthians tongues with ecstatic utterances also fits foreign languages which were not learned by the speaker and not understood by the hearers. Why would anyone suggest the interpretation of ecstatic utterances if it were not to give credibility to a psychological phenomenon which they do not understand? The explanation of the glossolalia experiences of today are to be found in abnormal psychology, not in the New Testament.

Pagan Ecstasy

There are many similarities between pagan ecstatic speech and contemporary glossolalia.[16] E. R. Dodds describes the Apollo oracle at Delphi:

> *At Delphi, and apparently at most of his oracles, Apollo replied, not on visions like those of Theoclymenus, but on "enthusiasm" in its original and literal sense. The Pythis became enteos, plena deo: the god entered into her and used her vocal organs as if they were his own, exactly as the so-called "control" does in modern spirit-mediumship.*[17]

16. James D. Bales, Pat Boone and the Gift of Tongues (Searcy, Arkansas: James D. Bales, 1970). pp. 62f
17. E. R. Dodds, The Greeks and the Irrational (Boston: Beacon Press, 1957) pp. 70-71.

The names of the gods have changed but the claims of the devotees are the same between the ancient Apollo cult and the modern advocates of glossolalia. Both claim to be possessed by God. Both claim that God takes over the vocal cords. Both obtain this state in the context of religious devotion. Both have total faith in the utterance that comes from such a state.

The Dionysus mystery cult had a similar phenomenon. E. R. Dodds describes this religion also.

> *If I understand early Dionysiac ritual right, its social function was essentially cathartic, in the psychological sense: it purged the individual of those infectious irrational impulses which, when dammed up, had given rise, as they have done in other cultures, to outbreaks of dancing mania and similar manifestation or collective hysteria.* [18]

He further states that Dionysus was essentially a god of joy and accessible to all of every class. He was the god . . .

> *. . . who by very simple means, or by other means not so simple, enables you for a short time to stop being yourself, and thereby sets you free . . . . "Dionysus leads people on to behave madly"-which could mean anything from "letting yourself go" to becoming "possessed." The aim of his cult was ecstasis--which again could mean anything from "taking you out of yourself" to a profound alteration of personality.* [19]

Notice the similarities between this pagan mystery cult and the experiences reported by the modern glossolalists. Both purge the individual of deep tensions within the personality. Both make the individual "stop being himself." Both lead

18. Ibid., p. 76
19. Ibid., pp. 76-77

people to irrational behavior. Both make profound alterations in personality.

The question that must be answered is this. In what way are the basic external manifestations of these ancient religions different from the external manifestations of those who practice glossolalia today? Another problem exists. If the Corinthians gift of "tongues" was no more than a repetition of a phenomenon found in paganism, there was nothing distinctive about it. If there was nothing distinctive about the gift of "tongues" when compared with the pagan cults at Corinth, then how could it be a sign to confirm the gospel message?

It is a mistake to try to read an irrational, subjective, psychological phenomenon into the reasonable objective and practical gift of speaking in tongues in the early church. If ecstatic utterances are read into the interpretation of I Corinthians 12-14, they would destroy the purpose of the miraculous gifts in the New Testament. What would be unique about Christians speaking in ecstatic utterances in Corinth when the same thing was going on in pagan cults in the city? If, however, the Christians at Corinth were speaking in other languages by a miraculous gift, this would be unique. This would be something that the mystery cults could not do.

There is nothing in the New Testament which demands that *glossa* "tongues" be understood as ecstatic utterance. One should not try to press such an interpretation--against the weight of evidence to the contrary--in order to try to give credibility to an experience they do not understand. Instead of trying to make the *glossa* gift of the New Testament conform to a present-day psychological phenomenon, accept it for what it really was--a unique gift given to Christians in the early church to speak in languages which they had not learned.

Most contemporary glossolalists agree that their speech is

language of a sort. James Ash writes:

> . . . *One of the marked characteristics of the modern movement is an emphatic denial that glossolalia is ecstatic in the sense of being emotionally enduced.* [20]

The question that must be answered is how can that contemporary phenomenon be distinguished from the ecstatic utterances common in paganism and world religions today?

The New Testament gift was language. If glossolalists today possess this same gift, it would be simple to identify it. Modern communication and transportation could take tapes of glossolalia speech around the world to be examined by the greatest language experts.

A number of recent studies have been made of the glossolalia speech, but none indicate that the speech is "language" unknown to the speaker. [21] If glossolalia speech is not foreign languages, let its advocates go outside the New Testament for their authority. It is not from God. Bob Cannon writes:

> *Do those who claim this gift today have what the New Testament Christians had? If not, then they must look for other validation for their "experiences." The New Testament is not their authority.* [22]

20. James L. Ash, "A Critique of Restorationist Pneumatology" (unpublished paper, January, 1971), p. 6.

21. E. Mansell Pattison, "Behavioral Science Research on the Nature of Glossolalia," Journal of American Scientific Affiliaton 20:3, (September, 1968).

22. Bob Cannon, Glossolalia (privately published tract), p. 24.

CHAPTER 4

PURPOSE OF THE NEW TESTAMENT GIFT

If the *glossa* gift in the New Testament were languages, then what was its purpose? This has been one of the knotty problems with which Bible scholars have long wrestled.

A Tool of Evangelism

It is quite doubtful that the purpose of the *glossa* gift was primarily to help the early Christians in evangelizing the world. It would have been quite convenient for them to have known different languages in their evangelizing. The evidence, however, does not show this.

One might think that the circumstances on Pentecost might argue for this interpretation. After all, this was when the gospel was preached for the first time. It was preached to a multilanguaged audience. It was understood by each nationality in his own native language. No one can deny that this gift of languages was helpful in this situation. But was it the primary purpose of the gift? Most of those present on Pentecost could probably have understood Greek and/or Aramaic. It would seem unnecessary for all fifteen languages to have been spoken if it were merely an evangelistic tool.

The gift of languages was not prominent in the early church after Pentecost. One of the first problems in the church arose because Grecian widows were being neglected in the daily ministration of goods. Neglected Grecians in a Jewish city might suggest a communication problem. The gift of tongues was not needed to solve the problem--only qualified men.

Two things argue against the interpretation that its purpose was a tool of evangelism.

First, Paul did not see the gift of languages at Corinth as helping them in evangelism. If an outsider would come to their assemblies when the Corinthian Christians were speaking in tongues, they would not understand the speech and think them mad. Instead of the gift of languages being a help in evangelism, it would be a hinderance in this situation.

Second, there is no statement in the New Testament that would indicate that this was the purpose of the gift of language. In the travels of Paul, there would have been ample opportunity for Luke to have mentioned how his gift of language helped him to preach the gospel in strange lands. He never mentioned such. The silence is very forceful in this situation.

It would appear that there was a greater purpose for the gift than just expediting the communication process.

A Language of Ecstasy

There is no indication that the purpose of the *glossa* gift was to furnish a "language of ecstasy" or a "heavenly prayer language" to be used in private devotion. Such was unknown to the early Christians.

One must accept glossolalia today as valid experience for the individual who is caught up in the practice. The question is this, IS THE EXPERIENCE FROM GOD OR MAN? Is the practice of such ecstasy language to be found in the New Testament or is it merely a human psychological phenomenon?

The New Testament *glossa* gift had three characteristics:

First, the utterance came from the Holy Spirit. That is, the person who had the gift did not have to think what he was to say. In this way it was like prophecy. It was different from prophecy in that it was a foreign language while prophecy was in the native tongue. Jesus promised his apostles that the Spirit would take control and guide them in their speech when they were on trial.

> *But when they deliver you up, be not anxious how or what ye shall speak: for it shall be given you in that hour what ye shall speak. For it is not ye that speak, but the Spirit of your Father that speaketh in you.*[1]

The Holy Spirit also took control when one spoke in tongues in the New Testament. Luke records: *"And they were all filled with the Holy Spirit and began to speak with other tongues as the Spirit gave them utterance."*[2]

Second, the Spirit did not so overwhelm the individual so that he lost control of his speech. Those who possessed the gift were able to speak in a foreign language by the power of the the Holy Spirit. The time and place for exercising the gift was in control of the possessor. This is shown by Paul's instruction to the church at Corinth concerning the use of the *glossa* gift.

> *If any man speaketh in a tongue, let it be by two, or at the most three, and that in turn; and let one interpret: but if there be no interpreter let him keep silence in the church.*[3]

The individual was always in control of the gift. If not, the

1. Matthew 10:19-20.
2. Acts 2:4.
3. I Corinthians 14:27-28a.

directions by Paul were meaningless. The individual could use his will and take turns with others who possessed the gift. He could use his will and decide not to speak in tongues if no interpreter were present.

Speaking in tongues, like the gift of prophecy, could be controlled by the speaker. Paul said: *"The spirit of the prophets are subject to the prophets."*[4]

Third, the gift of tongues was for edification. It was to edify both the hearer and the speaker. Those who possessed the gift at Corinth were not exercising the gift in this way. They were not using the gift to edify the church, but to satisfy their own selfish pride.[5]

Paul said that prophecy is better than tongues because the church is edified by prophecy:

He that speaketh in a tongue edifieth himslef; but he that prophesieth edifieth the church . . . greater is he that prophesieth than he that speaketh with tongues, except he interpret, that the church may receive edifying.[6]

He gave further instructions that tongues were not to be used in the meeting of the church unless there was an interpreter.

Those at Corinth who exercised the gift did not always

4. I Corinthians 14:32.
5. The question is posed here of how one can suggest that the Holy Spirit would assist one in satisfying his own selfish pride. This is the point Paul makes in I Corinthians 12-14. The possessors of the gift were not correctly using the gift. They were abusing it. The gift of God's grace does not guarantee the perfection of man's will. Man can abuse as well as use the gifts of God. Balaam did in Numbers 22-24. Paul shows the Corinthians were also abusing the gift of prophecy in I Corinthians 14:29-33.
6. I Corinthians 14:4, 5b.

understand what they were saying. They did not seem to care. They were so caught up in the showiness of the gift that they neglected to see its real purpose. Paul corrected this error:

> *Wherefore let him that speaketh in a tongue pray that he may interpret. For if I pray in a tongue, my spirit prayeth, but my understanding is unfruitful. What is it then? I will pray with the spirit and I will pray with the understanding also. I will sing with the spirit,. and I will sing with the understanding also.*[7]

The one speaking in tongues should not leave out his own understanding. He should seek to understand and translate the message he has spoken in another language.

God does not want "tape recorders" worshipping him. He wants persons. God is not served by empty noises that come from passive matter. He wants service from the heart--the mind--the understanding of men. Jesus said: *"The hour cometh and now is, when the true worshipers shall worship the Father in spirit and truth; for such doth the Father seek to be his worshipers."*[8] God is not being worshipped by an individual who gives forth utterance that neither he nor others understand. This makes man a mere mechanical instrument. Jesus applied a prophecy from Isaiah to the scribes and Pharisees of his day in his condemnation of their vain worship. The same passage applies to those who seek to worship God with their lips; but without understanidng: *"This people honoreth me with their lips; but their heart is far from me."*[9]

Trying to worship God without knowing what you are saying is dangerous. How does one know whether he is praising

7. I Corinthians 14:13-15.
8. John 4:23.
9. Matthew 15:8 .

God or cursing God? This was the question posed by Paul in I Corinthians 12:2-3:

> *Ye know that when ye were Gentiles ye were led away unto those dumb idols, howsoever ye might be led. Wherefore I make known unto you, that no man speaking in the Spirit of God saith, Jesus is anathema: and no man can say, Jesus is Lord, but in the Holy Spirit.*

If an individual does not know what he is saying and his listeners do not know what he is saying, how can it be known if his ecstatic utterances are praising Jesus or cursing Jesus? It is a dangerous thing to surrender one's will to some power outside himself and utter things he does not understand. The Holy Spirit is not the only spirit which tries to work in man. There are also unholy spirits. Unholy spirits say Jesus is anathema. The Holy Spirit says Jesus is Lord. If one does not know what he is saying, how can he tell whether the spirit be Holy or unholy?

It is true that a Christian sometimes has feelings of devotion and praise that are too deep for words. Sometimes love is so great that it cannot be expressed in language. Sometimes joy is so full that all the words of men are inadequate. It is also true that the Holy Spirit helps the Christian in communicating these deep feelings of his heart to God. Paul says:

> *The Spirit also helpeth our infirmity: for we know not how to pray as we ought: but the Spirit himself maketh intercession for us with groanings which cannot be uttered; and he that searcheth the hearts knoweth what is the mind of the Spirit, because he maketh intercession for the saints according to the will of God.*[10]

When the Spirit intercedes for the Christian before God, it is

---

10. Romans 8:26-27.

not with ecstatic utterances. It is with unutterable groaning. Paul is specific here and says it is not by speech--whether known or unknown. The RSV translates the phrase as "sighs too deep for words." Although one might not understand what all is involved in this intercession of the Spirit, he can know that it does not refer to the glossolalia experience today. Glossolalia is characterized with utterable sounds.

The New Testament gift was not "heavenly prayer language" as claimed by some glossolalists today. It does not fit the evidence.

Three Purposes of the Glossa Gift

There are three purposes of the *glossa* gift given in the New Testament.

The first and most evident is the confirmation of the new revelation of God spoken by inspired men. God gave a new revelation for man on the day of Pentecost. It was confirmed to be from God because of the signs which accompanied the new revelation. This was the promise made to those who first preached the gospel: *"These signs shall accompany them that believe . . . . They shall speak with new tongues."*[11] Mark said that this promise was fulfilled in the work of the apostles: *"And they went forth, and preached everywhere, the Lord working with them, and confirming the word by the signs that followed."*[12]

It is natural for men to question new revelation from God. The question is asked. Is the revelation really from God? Perhaps it is just the man's own ideas. Perhaps it is a delusion of

11. Mark 16:17.
12. Mark 16:20.

the devil. How can one know for sure? By signs! The One who empowered his servants to work signs and miracles is the Person who has the authority to give new revelation. God has always given signs with new revelation. Moses had them. The judges had them. The prophets had them. The New Testament writers had them.

This truth is confirmed by Hebrews 2:1-4. The author encourages his readers to give heed to the word which was first spoken by the Lord and was confirmed by those who heard. The author further says that God was also *"bearing witness with them, both by signs and wonders, and by manifold powers, and by gifts of the Holy Spirit."* That which was spoken by the Lord was confirmed by both the apostles' witness and by signs. The message received its sanction as being from God by the bearers of the message working signs.

This principle of new revelation being confirmed with signs is demonstrated on the day of Pentecost. Peter and the other apostles had new revelation to proclaim. God bore witness to this new revelation with signs--of which one was the gift of tongues. One of Peter's proofs that his message concerning the resurrected Jesus was true is recorded in Acts 2:33: *"Being therefore by the right hand of God exalted, and having received of the Father the promise of the Holy Spirit, he hath poured forth this, which ye see and hear."* The new revelation was confirmed by signs which were seen and heard.

If the gift of tongues and other signs are still worked by the power of God, where is the new revelation? If there is no new revelation, then how can these signs be from God? The Mormons are consistent on this point. They have always claimed the "gift of tongues" and other signs. They also claim new revelation confirmed by these signs. The Book of Mormon is a part of this new revelation. It is supposed to be from God.

They claim the signs from God--like "speaking in tongues"--confirm it. If their signs are from God, so is their revelation. If their revelation is not from God, neither are their signs. They stand or fall together.

This poses a difficult problem for the glossolalists today. If the glossolalia experience is really from God--then so is the "tongue speaking" claimed by the Mormons. If the "tongue speaking" of the Mormons is from God--then so is their new revelation, the Book of Mormon. The present day glossolalist is put into the position of accepting the Book of Mormon if they accept the Mormon glossolalia experience as being from God.

A second purpose of the *glossa* gift in the New Testament was for edification. The gift could edify if it were spoken to an audience who knew the language that was being spoken. This happened on the day of Pentecost.[13] The gift could also edify when it was used in the presence of an interpreter.[14] The gift was not to be used unless it would edify. This was the instruction that Paul laid down in the Corinthian church.[15] It would appear that this edifying purpose of the *glossa* gift was a secondary purpose. The primary purpose was that of confirmation as laid down by Jesus.

A third purpose can be discovered for the *glossa* gift by the way it was being used in the church at Corinth. Paul said:

> *Wherefore tongues are for a sign, not to them that believe, but to the unbelieving. But prophesying is for a sign not to the unbelieving, but to them that believe. If therefore the whole church be assembled together*

13. Acts 2:1-11.
14. I Corinthians 14:27-28.
15. I Corinthians 14:26.

*and all speak with tongues, and there come in men un-
learned or unbelieving, will they not say that ye are
mad?*[16]

The *glossa* gift, as it was being used at Corinth, was a sign to
the unbelieving.

Tongues are not a sign to them that believe. First, they do
not need a sign. Paul had already told the Corinthians it
was not signs but preaching "Christ crucified" that leads men
to salvation.[17] The Jews wanted signs but Paul preached
Christ. Believers do not need signs. Believers do not tempt
God by trying to make God cater to their whims any more
than Jesus would tempt God by casting himself down from
the temple.[18] Second, believers prefer prophesying over
tongues. They are more concerned with being edified than being amazed. Paul said, *"prophesying is a sign . . . to them that
believe."*

Tongues are not a sign for the unbelieving and unlearned of
the world. Paul showed this by using an illustration from the
life of the church. The whole church--Corinthian Christians--
assembled and spoke in tongues. Then an outsider--one unbelieving and unlearned--comes into the assembly while this
glossa gift was being exercised. There is confusion and it appears that the church is made up of mad men. The *glossa* gift
would not help him to become a believer. He could not understand the *glossa* gift because he was "unlearned." He could not
understand that it was a charismatic gift of the Holy Spirit because he was an "unbeliever." Instead of producing faith, it
would hinder faith.

On Pentecost the *glossa* gift was helpful to the "unbeliever"

16. I Corinthians 14:22-23.
17. I Corinthians 1:18-23.
18. Matthew 4:5-7.

since they understood in their own language. In situations where the *glossa* gift was not understood it would not be helpful to "unbelievers."

"Tongue speaking" is not an evangelistic tool for converting those who do not understand what is being said. It is a hindrance rather than a help. Prophecy should be used to teach the unlearned and the unbelieving. Paul says:

> *If all prophesy, and there come in one unbelieving or unlearned, he is reproved by all, he is judged by all; the secrets of his heart are made manifest; and so he will fall down on his face and worship God, declaring that God is among you indeed.*[19]

To whom then are tongues a sign? To unbelieving people of God who reject the plain and edifying prophecy. The abuse of the *glossa* gift brought a change of its primary purpose. Tongue speaking to the Corinthians was not a sign of their faith, it was a sign of unbelief. They like the unbelieving priests and prophets of Isaiah's day had rejected plain prophecy.[20] Men of strange tongues were to come to Jerusalem and be heard by the unbelieving priests and prophets in Isaiah's day as a testimony of their refusing to hear plain prophecy. Just so, the strange tongues of those who possessed the *glossa* gift at Corinth were a testimony of their refusal to give heed to plain prophecy.[21]

Paul sees one of the purposes of tongues as a sign to the unbelieving people of God who placed edifying prophecy in a secondary position. This purpose is no doubt secondary since the primary purpose as given by Jesus seemed to be that of

19. I Corinthians 14:24-25.

20. J. P. M. Sweet, "A Sign For Unbelievers," New Testament Studies, XIII (April, 1971), p. 242.

21. See pages 132ff.

confirming new revelation. Paul used this secondary purpose of the gift of tongues to show the unbelief of those who preferred tongue speaking to plain prophecy. Perhaps this says something to those who prefer a counterfeit "gift of tongues" to plain prophecy in the Scriptures today.

The Glossa Gift and the Present

Phenomenon Contrasted

The New Testament "gift of tongues" is quite different from the present practice of glossolalia. Chapter one describes the present phenomenon as ecstatic utterances and shows them to be strictly a human psychological experience. Chapters two, three and four describe the New Testament "gift of tongues" and show that it was a miraculous sign to confirm new revelation brought through Jesus Christ. Notice the contrast between the *glossa* gift of the New Testament and contemporary glossolalia.

1. The New Testament gift was the gift of foreign language. The present phenomenon is nothing more than ecstatic utterances known in all world religions, ancient and modern, and sometimes outside of religion altogether.

2. The New Testament gift was to be used to edify the church. The present phenomenon is claimed for personal elation and private devotion.

3. The New Testament gift was received either through the baptism of the Holy Spirit or by the imposition of apostles' hands. The present phenomenon is received by certain types of persons who have an intense personal desire for the gift.

4. The New Testament gift could be understood by men who know the language. The present phenomenon is not understood by linguists.[22]

5. The New Testament gift, along with the other miraculous gifts was used to confirm new revelation. The present phenomenon has no new revelation to confirm.

6. The New Testament gift was temporary and those who possessed the gift predicted that it would cease. Those who experience the present phenomenon claim that the glossolalia experience is an abiding gift for Christians of all ages.

22. Certain foreign phrases are thought to be heard in some glossolalia experiences, but these can be psychologically explained and are not to be compared with the clear gift of foreign language in the New Testament.

SECTION II

CHAPTER 5

HISTORICAL MENTION OF GLOSSOLALIA

It is not the purpose of the author to give a detailed history of the glossolalia experience in this one short chapter. Fuller historical discussions may be found in other places.[1] The author has only included material which he believes has important bearing on the subject. There could be a multiplying of evidence. This is unnecessary. The material contained in this chapter is representative of a larger body of evidence which is to be found throughout the history of religion and the history of Christianity in particular.

The study of the history of glossolalia can be quite helpful in understanding it. It will show four things. (1) It is not a new phenomenon, but has been known throughout the history of Christianity after the first century. (2) It is not a phenomenon known only in Christianity, but is also common in ancient pagan as well as modern world religion. (3) It has generally been associated with heresy in Christianity and often as evidence of new revelation beyond the Scriptures. (4) It has arisen during times of great stress and/or at a time when the established religion had grown dead and ritualistic.

Ancient Paganism

There are many instances of the glossolalia phenomenon

---

1. See Morton T. Kelsey. Tongue Speaking (New York: Doubleday and Co., 1964); and George Barton Cutten, Speaking with Tongues (New Haven: Yale University Press, 1927).

in paganism.   As has already been shown, ecstatic speech was one of the prominent features of the Apollo cult at Delphi and the Dionysus mystery cult.[2]   Ecstatic utterance and other experiential practices played an important role in both the native Greek religions and the mystery cults which they imported from the East.   Dodds sees these religions which emphasized the irrational as a necessity in Greek culture.   He writes:

> *In a guilt-culture, the need for supernatural assurance, for an authority transcending man's appears to be overwhelmingly strong . . . without Delphi, Greek society could scarcely have endured the tensions to which it was subjected in the Archaic Age.*[3]

The essential function of such experiences, according to Dodd, was cathartic.[4]   These irrational experiences gave an escape from the tensions of the culture.

One of the earliest accounts of this ecstasy experience is that of Wen-Amon in Byblos in 1100 B. C. He was from Egypt and had traveled to Byblos on the Palestine coast.   Pritchard translates the account thus:

> *Now while he was making offerings to his gods, the god seized one of his youths and made him possessed.   And he said to him: "Bring up the god." Bring the messenger who is carrying him." Amon is the one who sent him out." He is the one who made him come." And while the possessed youth was having his frenzy on this night, I had already found a ship headed for Egypt.*[5]

2. See page 42f.
3. E. R. Dodds.   The Greeks and the Irrational (Boston: Beacon Press, 1957), p. 75.
4. Ibid., p. 76.
5. James B. Pritchard.   Archaeology and the Old Testament (Princeton: Princeton University Press, 1959), p. 80.

This account does not specify that the youth spoke in ecstatic speech, only that he was in a frenzy. It should be noted
that it was the god who was speaking through him and that
he was possessed by the god.

Plato wrote in several places about Divine madness. He believed that the poet, the prophetess at Delphi, the priestess at
Dodona and the Sibyl all possessed a madness brought on by
the gods. Plato believed that the ecstatic speaking which was
carried on during these ecstasies benefited the state:

> *We owe our greatest blessings to madness, if only it be
> granted by Heaven's bounty. For the prophetess at Del-
> phi, ye are well aware, and the priestesses of Dodna, have
> in their moments of madness done great and glorious
> service to men and the cities of Greece, but little or none
> in their sober mood.*[6]

Plato believed that the inspiration that comes to poets also
comes by irrational means from the gods:

> *Herein lies the reason why the Diety has bereft them of
> their senses, and uses them as ministers, along with sooth-
> sayers and godly seers: it is in order that we listeners
> may know that it is not they who utter these precious
> revelations while their mind is not within them, but that
> it is the God himself who speaks.*[7]

Ecstatic utterance claiming to come from God is not a modern
thing. Neither is it confined to the limits of historical Christianity. An incident claiming to be a divine sign ceases to be a
sign when it is shown to be a commonplace occurrence. It
ceases to be regarded as divine when it is shown to be brought

6. J. Wright (trans.), Dialogues of Plato (New York: A. L. Burt Co.,
n.d.), pp. 34-35.
7. Lane Cooper (trans.), Plato (New York: Oxford University Press,
1948), pp. 83-84.

on by strictly human means.

Christianity After 150 A. D.

One striking thing stands out in the study of the literature of the "apostolic fathers." There is no evidence that Christians practiced "speaking in tongues" in the post-apostolic age. writings of the first century would have mentioned such a phenomenon if such existed. Their silence on this subject speaks loud and clear that such experiences were not a part of the church during the first hundred years of its existence.

Jack McKinney writes:

> *Several years ago while doing graduate study in the writings of the "apostolic fathers," I was impressed with the fact that evidence of charismatic gifts, excepting visions and possibly prophetic inspiration, was sparse Neitheir tongues nor healings are to be found.* [8]

In the first century men were too close to the genuine apostolic gift to allow the ecstatic utterance that characterized the pagan cults. After the death of apostolic men the *glossa* gift of the New Testament ceased. The writers in the church during the first and early part of the second century point to this fact by their silence.

Writers began to mention the "gift of tongues" again in the middle of the second century. The first mention is probably found in Irenaeus:

> *For this reason does the apostle declare, "we speak wisdom among them that are perfect," terming those persons "perfect" who have received the Spirit of God, and*

8. Jack McKinney, "From Sinai to Jerusalem," (unpublished paper, January, 1971), p. 3.

who through the Spirit of God do speak in all languages,
as he used himself also to speak. In like manner we do
also hear (or have heard) many brethren in the Church
who possess prophetic gifts, and who through the Spirit
speak all kinds of languages.[9]

It is difficult to determine from this passage whether Irenaeus
had actually heard men speak in "all kinds of languages" by
the Spirit or whether it was something about which he had
only heard. Nor does the passage indicate whether the
"brethren" who possessed the gift were Montanists. In either
case it is known that there were those in the days of Irenaeus
who were reputed to possess the gift. It should also be noted
that Irenaeus does not even mention the "gift of tongues"
when he lists the gifts of the Holy Spirit earlier in the same
work.[10]

The claim of the "gift of tongues" was common among
the Montanists. This heretical group was named for Montanus
(c. A. D. 156), who was a priest of Cybele before his conversion. He would reach a state of ecstasy and gave forth utterances. These utterances were supposed to be oracles of God.
Montanus claimed that the Holy Spirit spoke directly through
him.

Tertullian was a prominent spokesman of the Montanists.
He gives evidence of "tongue-speaking" among them in a passage he wrote against Marcion:

Let Marcion then exhibit, as gifts of his god, some pro-
phets, such as have not spoken by human sense, but with
the Spirit of God, such as have predicted things to
come, and have made manifest the secrets of the heart:

---

9. A Cleveland Coxe, "The Apostolic Fathers," The Ante-Nicene
Fathers, Vol. I., eds. Alexander Roberts and James Donaidson (New
York: Charles Scribner's Sons, 1899), p. 444.
10. Ibid., I, p. 409.

let him produce a psalm, a vision, a prayer--only let it be by the Spirit, in an ecstasy, that is, in a rapture, whenever an interpretation of tongues has occurred to him . . . . Now all these signs (of spiritual gifts) are forthcoming from my side without any difficulty.[11]

It should be noted that Tertullian understood the "gift of tongues" to have an apologetic value. They were proof that the possessor spoke for God. The Montanists had new revelatoin and these gifts that they claimed to possess was proof that their new revelation came from God.

Origen makes no mention of "tongue speaking" being within the church. He does condemn a similar phenomenon that was found in the contemporary religions of his day:

There are many who, although of no name, with the greatest facility and on the slightest occasion, whether within or without temples, assume the motions and gestures of inspired persons; while others do it in cities or among armies, for the purpose of attracting attention and exciting surprise . . . . To these promises are added strange, fanatical, and quite unintelligible words, of which no rational persons can find the meanings for so dark are they, as to have no meaning at all; but they give occasion to every fool or imposter to apply them to suit his own purposes.[12]

The refutation made by Origen against the "experiential religions" of his day could very aptly be applied to similar situations in our own times. Is attracting attention and exciting surprise one of the purposes of glossolalia? There can be no question that strange, fanatical unintelligible words give opportunity for imposters, under the guise of interpretation, to use

11. Ibid., III, p. 447.
12. Ibid., IV., p. 614.

them to their own selfish ends.

Origen was the first to put forth the interpretation that the "gift of tongues" on Pentecost was a permanent endowment of knowledge of foreign languages for the use of taking the gospel to foreign lands.[13] It should also be noted that he considered the "tongues" in Corinth also to be a foreign language.[14]

In the fourth century there is mention of a certain Pacomius, an Egyptian, who was supposed to have spoken Greek and Latin without having learned them.[15] The incident was told by a monk who was writing the story of Pacomius' life.

Gregory of Nazianzen also comments concerning the gift of tongues on Pentecost. He points to the fact that the *glossa* gift was considered as languages. He says, *"They spoke with strange tongues and not their native languages, a language spoken by those who had not learned it."*[16]

It was Gregory of Nyssa, also in the fourth century, who first contrasted the speaking in foreign languages on Pentecost with the confusion of langauges at the tower of Babel.[17]

Chrysostom, still in the fourth century, was the first to refer to the cessation of the *glossa* gift.[18] He, like Gregory of Nyssa, connected the Pentecost event to the tower of Babel. He understood the gift to be the gift of languages. In commenting

13. Dawson Walker, The Gift of Tongues (Edinburgh: T and T Clark, 1906), p. 16.

14. Ibid.

15. Cobham Brewer, A Dictionary of Miracles (London: Chatto and Windus, 1897), p. 154.

16. Charles Gordon Brown, James Edward Shallo (trans.) "Gregory" Nicene and Post-Nicene Fathers, Vol. VIII, eds. Philip Schaff and Henry Mace. (New York: The Christian Literature Co., 1906), p. 384.

17. Walker, op. cit., p. 18.

18. Ibid., p. 19.

on I Corinthians 12-14, he said:

> *This whole place is very obscure; but the obscurity is produced by our ignorance of the facts referred to and by their cessation, being such as then used to occur but now no longer take place.*[19]

Two things are clear from this statement. (1) He regarded that the *glossa* gift was difficult to understand. (2) He understood that the gift had ceased and was not being exercised during his time.

Ash in attempting to defend contemporary glossolalia makes a point of the fact that Chrysostom was the first to mention the cessation of the *glossa* gift. He writes:

> *Not until Chrysostom do we get the sub-dispensational interpretation. Is it reasonable to believe that Chrysostom, writing in the late fourth century, is more qualified to tell us what Paul meant than all the writers in the previous two centuries who consistently interpret "the perfect" eschatologically? If Paul meant what Chrysostom said he did, should we not expect somebody to articulate it before 300 years had passed and Chrysostom came on the scene? I can only conclude that the sub-dispensational theory was devised hundreds of years after Paul wrote I Corinthians, that it was motivated, then and now, by a defensive posture within an anemic and apostate church, and that it ought to be thoroughly repudiated by those who consider the first century apostles' doctrines authoritative . . . .*
> . . . .
> *A more recent work by G. W. H. Lampe clearly shows that the view that miracles have ceased belongs to the period of the later apologists and specifically to Chrysostom, who wrote in the late fourth century. Why does*

19. As quoted by Anthony A. Hoekema, What About Tongue Speaking? (Grand Rapids: Wm. B. Erdmans Publishing Co., 1966), p. 16.

this doctrine not appear until the later fourth century?[20]

This author will not attempt to judge the motives of either those who accept the subdispensational interpretation or those who reject it. This prerogative belongs to God, not to this author or James Ash.

As to why the doctrine does not appear in the patristic writings before Chrysostom, this author does not know. Perhaps it did appear and has not been preserved. Perhaps there was no need to write about the passing of the gift of tongues. There are very few references to anything which can be understood as the gift of tongues in the early patristic writings. When it is mentioned, it is connected with the apostolic period, heresy like Montanism or as in the case of Irenaeus, unconfirmed hearsay. From the mention that is made in the patristic writings, it is clear that it was not the common practice. Opposition to Montanism by early patristic writers would naturally be along lines that were more prominently a part of their teaching. This author has been unable to find sufficient information among the early patristic writers to determine how they would interpret I Corinthians 13:8-13. It is difficult to see how Ash could suggest that "all" the writers in the two centuries before Chrysostom "consistently interpret 'the perfect' eschatologically."

It is interesting to note that what Ash calls the "subdispensational interpretation" is a quite old and widely accepted interpretation of I Corinthians 13:8-13.[21] It was not read into the text as a polemic against contemporary glossolalists.

20. James L. Ash, "A Critique of Restorationist Pneumatology" (unpublished paper, January, 1971), p. 4, 2.

21. William Webster and William Francis Wilkinson, The Greek New Testament, Vol. II (London: Parker, Son and Bourn, 1861), pp. 266-67.

Neither is it a devisive scneme of an anemic and apostate church. Such an interpretation is an attempt of scholars to understand the passage.

Augustine agreed with Chrysostom on this interpretation. He said:

> In the earliest times, "the Holy Ghost fell upon them that believed: and they spake with tongues, "which they had not learned, "as the Spirit gave them utterances." These were signs adapted to the time. For there behooved to be that betokening of the Holy Spirit in all tongues, to show that the gospel of God was to run through all tongues over the whole world. That thing was done for a betokening, and it passed away.[22]

The above evidence shows that after Irenaeus, the "gift of tongues" began to be mentioned in the writings of Christian authors. Often it was associated with heresy, particularly the Montanists who claimed "latter day revelation." Beginning with the fourth century, writers began to develop a commentary on the New Testament texts which mention the *glossa* gift. There is some indication, especially in Egypt, that there still existed the belief that the gift of languages could be had by men of great devotion. This view was not held by the known scholars.

Middle Ages

During the middle ages there are very few references in literature that deal with "tongue speaking." Cutten comments on this poverty of material:

> . . . in the Middle Ages the saints are said to have

22. Morton T. Kelsey, Tongue Speaking (New York: Doubleday and Company, 1964), p. 40.

received the gift and used it for speaking with people of other tongues in their missionary labor. It is rather surprising, however, that, in this age of wonders, it appears so infrequently.[23]

Brewer tells of St. Vincent Ferrier who spoke in his native dialect of Valencia and was understood by Greeks, Germans and Hungarians. He also relates the story of St. Louis Bertrand, who was supposed to have converted 30,000 South American Indians through the gift of tongues.[24] Brewer documents a number of other stories in which missionaries were supposed to have been endowed with the miraculous gift of languages.

As has already been noted, the Rituale Romanum, the official book of public services which dates around 1000 gives "use or knowledge of an unknown language" as being one of the signs of demon possession.[25] This would indicate that such glossolalia phenomenon was known during the Middle Ages. It was interpreted as possession by the devil rather than possession by the Holy Spirit in some parts of the Roman Catholic world.

In the eleventh century, the Greek Orthodox and the Roman Catholic churches went their separate ways. In Greek Orthodoxy, glossolalia was not condemned as demon possession. It was allowed, but relegated to the monastaries.

Reformation

During the Reformation, glossolalia was known among the

23. George B. Cutten, Speaking With Tongues (New Haven: Yale University Press, 1927), p.37
24. Brewer, loc. cit.
25. See page 15.

followers of Zwingli and certain Anabaptists.[26] Although Luther has been claimed as a glossolalist, the evidence points to the contrary.

Zwingli acknowledged glossolalia, but placed a somewhat different interpretation than do modern advocates. He writes:

> *The outward baptism of the Spirit is an external sign, the gift of tongues. This sign is not given for the benefit, of those who actually speak with other tongues or languages: for they have already learned the way of salvation in their hearts. It is given for the benefit of unbelievers . . . . And who are these? The ones to whom tongues are given? No, for they are already believers. They are given to believers as a sign and wonder to unbelievers . . . this outward baptism of tongues was appointed by the Lord himself in Acts 1: "Ye shall be baptized with the Holy Ghost not many days hence." Now the disciples were already believers. But the fire of love was increased and tongues were given as happened on the day of Pentecost. Again, this sign is not necessary to salvation, for it is given infrequently and only to a few. It is a miracle, and like other miracles it takes place only when God wills.[27]*

He regarded glossolalia as an external sign of the baptism of. the Holy Spirit. To him, it was the miraculous gift of languages that was given to the believer for a sign to the unbeliever. He did not regard the gift as necessary to salvation. It was rarely given and then only to a few. He does not indicate whether he possessed the gift himself or not.

---

26. Not all Anabaptists were enthusiasts. Too often Anabaptists are classified together even though different groups more radically differed from one another than they did from the established religion. This is particularly true on glossolalia. Some groups practiced it. Other groups disdained it.

27. G. W. Bromiley, Zwingli and Bullinger, The Library of Christian Classics, Vol. XXIV, eds. John Baillie, John T. McNeill and Henry P. Van Dusen (Philadelphia: The Westminster Press, 1953), pp. 137-38.

Williams tells of Anabaptists in St. Gall who practiced glossolalia along with other wild excesses. Children of seven and eight lay in a coma for hours. There was lewdness and unchastity. One woman said she was predestined to give birth to the Antichrist.[28] Other isolated incidents of glossolalia are to be found among the loosely knit and often contradictory Anabaptist groups.[29] Glossolalia, however, did not seem to hold a prominent place in the movement. It occurred in extreme groups and only in isolated circumstances.

Muntzer often identified as one of the Anabaptist leaders was a contemporary of Luther. He broke with Luther over the nature of religious authority. For Muntzer the Bible was not the source of faith, but only the guide to and the confirmation of the personal experience of the compulsive Spirit.[30] Muntzer, in his Sermon Before the Princes said:

> *This is now the character of almost all divines with mighty few exceptions. They teach and say that God no longer reveals his divine mysteries to his beloved friends by means of valid visions or his audible Word, etc. Thus they stick with their inexperienced way . . . and make into the butt of sarcasm those persons who go around in possession of revelation.*[31]

It was this dependence upon visions and revelations for religious authority that caused Luther and Muntzer to go separate ways. Bainton writes of this break: *"The real menace of Muntzer in Luther's eyes was that he destroyed the uniqueness*

28. George Hutston Williams, The Radical Reformation (Philadelphia: Westminister Press, 1952), p. 133.

29. Ibid., p. 443.

30. Geroge Williams and Angel Mergal, Spiritual and Anabaptist Writers, Vol. XXV of The Library of Christian Classics, eds., John T. McNeill and Henry P. Van Dusen; (Philadelphia: The Westministers Press, 1952), p. 32.

31. Ibid., p. 54.

of Christian revelation in the past by his elevation of revelation in the present.[32]

Luther has been claimed as a glossolalist.[33] The evidence does not bear out this claim. Luther and Muntzer's basic difference was over the nature of revelation. Luther held that it was Scripture only. Muntzer held that it was through visions and audible Word that men could understand the Bible. Thielicke writes of this difference:

> *Luther makes exactly the same point when in his controversy with the enthusiasts he emphasizes again and again the Holy Spirit is bound to the vehicle of the Word and that he reaches us only by means of this vehicle and not through free, unbound "blowing where he wills."*[34]

The emphasis that Luther placed on the Scriptures is the very thing which would argue against glossolalia, visions and revelations.

It is significant that there is so little mention of glossolalia in the Reformation. It was a time of great religious excitement. In the Anabaptist movement there were numerous claims of divine revelation, but little or no mention of glossolalia. Even in the Zwingli movement it does not find a prominent place.

Modern Times

After the Reformation period the glossolalia phenomenon continues to spring up at different periods. In the last part of the seventeenth century the French Huguenots produced "the

32. Roland H. Bainton, Here I Stand (New York: The New American Library of World Literature, Inc., 1950), p. 202.
33. Morton T. Kelsey, op. cit., p. 51.
34. Helmut Thielicke, Between Heaven and Earth (New York: Harper and Row, 1965), p. 95.

little prophets of Cevenes." The glossolalia phenomenon appeared among children. Sometimes whole groups would be caught up in the ecstasy. In the middle of the eighteenth century the French Catholic--Jansenists experienced numerous cases of glossolalia. Besides these there have been Quakers and Irvingites in England. More recently there have been Mormons and the Christian Missionary Alliance in the United States.

In the early nineteenth century religious awakening in the United States numerous religious exercises--including glossolalia--were quite common. Particularly was this the case in camp meetings on the American frontier. This phenomenon will be discussed later in the chapter on Mormonism.

The Pentecostal movement began in 1900 under the leadership of Charles Parham.[35] The place of origin was a Bible college in Topeka, Kansas. The movement spread rapidly through evangelistic efforts. Some of the leaders of the movement were .W. J. Seymour, C. H. Mason, C. P. Jones, Richard G. Spurling, A. J. Tomlinson and Aimee Semple McPherson.

In 1906 the headquarters of the movement was moved to Los Angeles under the leadership of Seymour. The location was an old livery stable on Azusa Street. Many Pentecostal groups look for their origin in this place. Aimee McPherson's temple in Los Angeles helped to spread the movement throughout the western part of the United States.

A mixture with an Armenian Pentecostal movement took place in 1906. A group migrating from Russia in the last part of the nineteenth century found its way to California and came into contact with the Azusa mission. Pentecostals have been

---

35. Vinson Synan, The Holiness Pentecostal Movement (Grand Rapids: Eerdmans, 1971). This is an excellent history of the Pentecostal movement.

called the "third force of Christendom." Within seventy years they have grown until they claim a membership of eight and a half million members.

A neo-Pentecostalism has arisen in the United States in the last ten years. Its origin has been traced to St. Mark's Episcopal Church in Van Nuys, California. The Rector Dennis Bennett first became involved in glossolalia. It then spread to the members of the church where he preached. It was at first bitterly opposed by the Episcopal religious authorities, but it spread like wildfire. In ten years, it has touched nearly every religious group in the United States.

One of the chief means of the spreading of this neo-Pentecostalism has been the Full Gospel Business Men's Fellowship International--FGBMFI. Oral Roberts helped in its organization in Los Angeles in 1960. Now there are chapters throughout the United States and in many parts of the world. Three of their magazines are Voice, Trinity and Testimony. Advocates of this neo-Pentecostalism include business executives, movie stars, T. V. personalities and college professors.

World Religions

Incidents of glossolalia can be multiplied from religions ancient and modern; eastern and western; established and heretical. The glossolalia experience is to be found in all different cultural strata from non-Christian priests to medicine men. The experience is to be found among the Hudson Bay Eskimos, North Boreno pagans, "demoniacs" in China and east Africa as well as Christianity. Burdick concludes:

This survey has shown that speaking-in-tongues is widespread and very ancient. Indeed, it is probably that as

*long as man has had divination, curing, sorcery, and pro-
pitiation of spirits, he has had glossolalia . . . . Whatever
the explanation, it is clear that pagans as well as Christians have their glossolalia experiences.*[36]

Comparative religious studies have shown that the Islam religion, like historical Christianity, has gone through periods of
rationalism and experientialism. Islam has a different Bible and
a different Christ from Christianity. The Moslem believes that
his Koran supercedes the New Testament and that Mohammed
supercedes Christ as God's prophet. The Moslem claims miracles. He believes that these miracles show God's favor and
confirms that correctness of his faith. Tongue speaking is one
of the miracles which is claimed. Hudjwiri describes the miraculous powers of an Islamic saint. He says that *"he can
transform himself, transport himself to a distance, speak diverse tongues, revive the dead. . . . "* [37] Other examples are
cited in Kenneth Morgan's book entitled, Islam the Straight
Path.[38]

Sufism arose in Islam in the eighth century. By then the
Islamic religion had degenerated into irrational intellectualism.
It, like so many other religions, had lost its spiritual content
through emphasis upon dogma and the dialectic. Sufism was a
reaction to this. The Sufis sought a knowledge of God--not
from the schools, but from direct personal experience. Gibb
writes:

*There was in their view, but one way to knowledge--
not the rational and secondhand "knowledge" ('ilm) of
the schools, but direct and personal "experience"*

36. Donald Burdick, Tongues, To Speak or Not to Speak (Chicago:
Moody Press, 1969), p. 67.
37. H. A. R. Gibb and J. H. Kramers, (eds.) Shorter Encyclopedia of
Islam (Ithaca, New York: Cornell University Press, n.d.), p. 629.
38. Kenenth W. Morgan, Islam the Straight Path (New York: Ronald
Press, 1958), p. 168.

(ma'rifa) culminating in momentary union or absorption into the Godhead.[39]

It is in this context that the "tongue speaking" experiences find their theological base.

Such subjective personal experiences, when found in non-Christian religions like Islam, present a practical problem to the glossolalist who claims to follow Jesus Christ. If a Christian finds religious validation in such subjective religious experiences, how can he reject the same kind of subjective religious experience in a Moslem who denies Jesus and rejects the Bible? Subjectivism is dangerous when it is used to validate religious truth. Bob Douglas writes:

> *When People begin to use their own experiences as a basis for verifying truth--as is done by those presently caught up in tongue-speaking movements--then religion is robbed of any objective standard. The problem becomes critical when we deal with world religions. If one accepts "tongue speaking" as proof of the Holy Spirit's presence in his life, how can he deal with the Moslem who claims to speak in "tongues" or to perform "miracles?" The Moslem also concludes that his abilities are God-given. He regards them as evidence of the truthfulness of the Islamic conclusions regarding Christ. This dilemma is beyond solution, until one returns the questions of authority to its rightful arena--objective truth which is the written Word of God. There is simply no logical way to reject these psychological phenomena which are a regular part of world religions--without objective truth.*[40]

Douglas' logic is clear. The glossolalist must face the fact that his experience is not unique. If his experience is really from God, then how are the experiences of the devoted Moslem to be explained?

---

39. H. A. R. Gibb, Mohammedanism (New York: Oxford University Press, 1962), p. 137.

40. Bob Douglas, "Biblical Authority in a Multireligious World," Star, 1:71 (January, 1971), p. 5.

CHAPTER 6

MORMONISM AND GLOSSOLALIA

A full chapter is given to Mormonism as it is related to glossolalia. There are three reasons for this. (1) Mormonism is a contemporary example of a religious group accepting experiences such as glossolalia as a part of its faith. In the doctrine and practice of Mormonism one is able to see the end results of religious presuppositions which allow for direct revelation from God. (2) Mormonism arose in the same cultural milieu as the Restoration Movement. Several leaders of the Restoration Movement also became leaders in Mormonism. Heirs of the Restoration Movement are able to see how glossolalia and its accompanying phenomenon of religious exercises were dealt with early in their history. (3) Mormonism has worked out its theology more fully and consistently than most other groups which practice glossolalia. This accounts for their acceptance of apostles, miracles, latter day revelation, etc. These are theological necessities when one accepts the direct operation of God and such things as glossolalia, healings and signs.

Roots in the Restoration Movement

Mormonism finds some of its roots in the Restoration Movement on the American frontier in the early nineteenth century. This is demonstrated in three ways.

First, Mormonism arose in the cultural milieu that was common to the Restoration Movement led by Alexander Campbell.

There was religious revival on the American frontier. It began about 1800 under the leadership of James McGready in northern Tennessee and southern Kentucky. Prominent in the revival was the Cane Ridge meeting in 1801 in which there were reported to be some 10,000 people in attendance--ten per cent of the entire white population of the state of Kentucky.

Garrison and DeGroot describe the revival thus:

> *As the revival interest grew, and as the meetings became larger and longer, unexpected and bizarre manifestations, called "exercises," began to occur. They were considered visible manifestations of the direct action of the Holy Spirit . . . . The commonest were the "falling exercise" and the "jerks." The names are sufficiently explanatory. The barking exercise sometimes accompanied the jerks, and the dancing exercise grew out of them. There was also the runnings exercise. It was reported that those who came to scoff were not immune to these seizures. However, it was only the devout who ever experienced the laughing exercise.*[1]

Among the exercises reported by Barton W. Stone in his autobiography was the "singing exercise." He writes:

> *This is more unaccountable than anything else I ever saw. The subject in a very happy state of mind would sing most melodiously, not from the mouth or nose, but entirely in the breast, the sounds issuing thence. Such music silenced everything and attracted the attention of all. It was most heavenly. None could ever be tired of hearing it. Dr. J. P. Campbell and myself were together at a meeting and were attending a pious lady thus exercised, and concluded it to be something surpassing anything we had known in nature.*[2]

1. Winfred E. Garrison and Alfred T. DeGroot, The Discliples of Christ (St. Louis: The Bethany Press, 1948), p. 99.
2. Ibid., p. 100.

Stone, leader of the Christians in the west who later joined with the Campbell movement, accepted these exercises as the mysterious acts of God which were beyond human understanding. There is no record of his ever participating in the exercises. But neither did they offend him nor did he discourage them.

Fawn Brodie tells of similar exercises which took place in the religious revival around the boyhood home of Joseph Smith, the founder of Mormonism in the mid 1820's:

Hundreds fell to the ground senseless, the most elegantly dressed women in Kentucky lying in the mud alongside ragged trappers. Some were seized with the "jerks," their heads and limbs snapping back and forth and their bodies grotesquely distorted. Those who caught the "barks" would crawl on all fours, growling and snapping like the camp dogs, fighting over garbage heaped behind tents . . . . One preacher wrote to another: "thousands of tongues with the sound of hallelujah seemed to run through infinite space; while hundreds of people lay prostrate on the ground crying for mercy. Oh! My dear brother, had you been there to have seen the convulsed limbs, the apparently lifeless bodies, you have been constrained to cry out as I was obliged to do, the gods are among the people." [3]

It was during the 1820's that the Restoration Movement was taking shape on the American frontier. During this same period and in the same area on the Western Reserve Mormonism found a fertile ground. This accounts for the similarity of expressions in the Book of Mormon and other early Mormon writings to the writings of leaders of the Restoration Movement like the Campbells, Walter Scott and Barton W. Stone.

3. Fawn M. Brodie, No Man Knows My History (New York: A. A. Knopf, 1945), p. 14.

The evangelistic tool of the "five steps of salvation" is common to the Mormons as well as the other heirs to the Restoration Movement. Joseph White writes:

> *Each group emphasizes and defines the terms as identically as possible, until the fifth step is reached (that being the gift of the Holy Ghost.) The Mormon divergence there is exactly the position that Rigdon preached, even after he was united with Disciples.*[4]

Second, some of the early influential leaders of Mormonism came from the ranks of the Restoration Movement. Sidney Rigdon, recognized by both Mormons and non-Mormons as having one of the greatest theological influences upon Mormon doctrine, was one time a preacher in the Restoration Movement. Parley Pratt, one of the original twelve apostles, was also a gospel preacher who went into Mormonism. Eliza Snow, plural wife of two prophets and poetess of Mormonism, was reared in a family active in the Restoration Movement around Kirtland, Ohio. The influence of these "Disciples turned Mormon" was to be felt throughout every aspect of Mormonism.

Third, it has been claimed, with the support of an impressive amount of evidence, that Sidney Rigdon was responsible for the religious contents of the Book of Mormon.[5] If this be true, one must see Mormonism as one of the streams of religious thought flowing out of the early Restoration Movement.

R. L. Roberts shows this in a article in the Star:

> *Rigdon's knowledge of the Book of Mormon prior to its*

4. Joseph W. White, The Influence of Sidney Rigdon Upon the Theology of Mormonism (an unpublished M. A. Thesis, University of Southern California, 1947), p. 68,

5. William Alexander Linn, The Story of the Mormons (New York: Russell and Russell Inc., 1963), pp. 59-73.

appearance can not be doubted if the testimony of such men as Adamson Bentley (Rigdon's brother-in-law), Campbell, Scott, and others in the churches where Rigdon preached before joining the new movement is true. Having been associated with these preachers of the churches of Christ from 1821, Rigdon was thoroughly familiar with Campbell's and Scott's ideas and expressions. When Scott saw the Book of Mormon and learned of Rigdon's acceptance of its claims, he recognized familiar phrases and expressions in the book. Naturally, he concluded that Rigdon was responsible for its religious content.[6]

Robert Richardson in his Memoirs of Alexander Campbell tells how Rigdon even before his conversion to Mormonism sought to privately convince influential people in the churches that supernatural gifts and miracles ought to be restored and all things should be held in common.[7]

Joseph White shows the dependency of Mormonism on restoration ideas. The bridge from one movement to the other was in the person of Sidney Rigdon. He writes:

This parallelism continues straight down the line of early Mormon doctrines. This fact is demonstrable. It also can be demonstrated that when Mormon doctrine did deviate, that the deviations were those which constantly kept Rigdon "in hot water" while he was with the Disciples.[8]

Sidney Rigdon was first a Baptist preacher. In 1820 he and Adamson Bentley visited Alexander Campbell. After discussing the Scriptures all night, Rigdon was convinced of the

6. R. L. Roberts, "Mormonism—An Example of Experiential Religion," Star, 1:71 (January 1971), p. 6.
7. Robert Richardson, Memoirs of Alexander Campbell (Philadelphia: J. B. Lippincott, 1868-70), Vol. II, p. 126.
8. Joseph White, loc. cit.

restoration principles and began to preach them on the Western Reserve.[9] Hayden calls him a "popular preacher" but said that he differed in emphasis from his fellow preachers. Richardson describes his ministry thus:

> . . . *(Rigdon) had for some time diligently engaged in endeavoring, by obscure hints and glowing millennial theories, to excite the imagination of his hearers, and in seeking by fanciful interpretations of Scripture to prepare the minds of the churches in Northern Ohio for something extraordinary in the near future.*[10]

It was in the area where Rigdon preached that Mormonism gained a following among the Disciples. Richardson estimates that one-half of the members of the church were led into Mormonism in Kirtland, Ohio.

Rigdon's preaching of "experiential religion" was soon rebuked by Alexander Campbell. Rigdon preached that the return to the "ancient order of things" included communism, divine healings, speaking in tongues, visions and revelations. Campbell's rebuke of Rigdon's preaching came about two or three months before the latter espoused Mormonism. Daryl Chase, a Mormon and Rigdon's chief biographer, wrote about the influence that Campbell's rebuke had upon Rigdon.

> *By accepting Mormonism, Rigdon got rid of the restraining hand of Alexander Campbell. He could move with greater freedom of speech, for the Mormons did not limit thier "restoration" ideas to the New Testament as had been the case with Campbell.*[11]

Campbell and Rigdon disagreed upon this basic point of

9. Amos Sutton Hayden, Early History of the Disciples in the Western Reserve (Cincinnati: Chase and Hall, 1875), p. 19.
10. Robert Richardson, op. cit., Vol. II, p. 346.
11. Daryl Chase, Sidney Rigdon—Early Mormon (an unpublished M. A. Thesis at the University of Chicago, 1931), p. 125.

authority. They could not long remain in the same fold. It was basically upon this point of authority that Mormons and members of churches of Christ have continued to disagree since that time.

Even before Rigdon turned to Mormonism, he believed in visions and revelations. After he left Mormonism, he still claimed to hear God's voice and enjoy the visitation of angels. Such experiential religious authority could not find a place in a movement that looked to Christ revealed in the Scriptures as their only authority.

Parley Pratt was another bridge between the two movements. He learned of the Campbell movement through the preaching of Rigdon and accepted it. Pratt, like Rigdon, felt he was miraculously directed by God. In his autobiography he writes of his "Divine-given experiences" which led him to Mormonism:

> . . . (I) felt drawn out in an extraordinary manner to search the prophets, and to pray for an understanding of the same . . . . I began to understand the things which were coming on the earth--the restoration of Israel, the coming of the Messiah, and the glory that should follow.[12]

After meeting Joseph Smith and accepting Mormonism in Palmyra, New York, Pratt returned with three other Mormon missionaries to Kirtland, Ohio. They were received by Rigdon and invited to preach. After two days, Rigdon was baptized into Mormonism. The following Sunday many in the church where Rigdon preached were also baptized into the new religion. John Doyle Lee in the book, Mormonism Unveiled, gives an account of this first Mormon meeting at Kirtland:

12. Parley P. Pratt, The Autobiography of Parley Parker Pratt (New York: Russell Brothers, 1874), p. 31.

*Many would have fits of speaking in all of the Indian
dialects which none could understand. Again at the dead
hour of night, young men might be seen running over
the fields and hills in pursuit, as they said, of balls of
fire, lights, etc.*[13]

Three weeks after Rigdon espoused Mormonism, he visited
Joseph Smith. Smith had a revelation that Rigdon was to be a
leader in the movement. Although Rigdon finally left Mormonism, his influence in the formative years of the religion was so
great that he is recognized as one of the true originators of the
movement. Pratt was to be an apostle. Mormonism and the
Restoration Movement are historically connected in the lives
and works of these two men along with Eliza Snow.

Difference on Authority

After noting the connections between the early Restoration
Movement, the next step is to see the point of difference. The
difference was on authority. Mormons accepted experiential
authority--including visions, tongues and revelations. Campbell and those in the Restoration Movement accepted the
Scriptures as their only guide. It was at this point that Rigdon
and Campbell disagreed. It was also at this point that the two
movements have gone their separate ways from a common cultural milieu on the American frontier.

Tongue speaking and its accompanying religious exercises
were physical expressions of experiential religions--opposed
by Campbell but espoused by Rigdon and others. Those in the
Restoration Movement who accepted the "direct work of the
Holy Spirit and these physical signs" were led into Mormonism. Those who did not, remained with churches of Christ.

13. John Doyle Lee, Mormonism Unveiled (Salt Lake City, Utah:
Modern Microfilm Co., n.d.) pp. 104-05.

Hayden writes that the climate was right for Mormonism when it came to the Western Reserve in 1830. He writes:

> . . . *many people, victims of excitement and credulity and taught in nearly all pulpits to pray for faith, now found themselves met on their own grounds, and so finding an emotion or impulse answerable to an expected response from heaven, dared not dispute the answer to their own prayer.*[14]

He further adds that Mormonism made no greater inroads among the disciples on the Western Reserve because of the basic difference in their view of authority:

> *The reason the delusions made little progress among the disciples save only at Kirtland where the way for it was paved by the common stock principle, is to be found in the cardinal principle everywhere taught and accepted among them that faith is founded upon testimony.*[15]

Tongue speaking has been a basic part of Mormonism from its beginning. The seventh Article of Faith in the Mormon Creed states, *"We believe in the gift of tongues, prophecy, revelation, visions, healing, interpretation of tongues, etc."* A statement in the Book of Mormon shows how closely Mormon theology connects tongue-speaking and new revelation:

> *And again I speak unto you who deny the revelations of God, and say that they are done away, that there are no revelations, nor prophecies, nor gifts, nor healing, nor speaking with tongues, and the interpretation of tongues: behold I say unto you, he that denieth these things knoweth not the gospel of Christ.*[16]

14. Amos Sutton Hayden, op. cit., p. 216.
15. Ibid., p. 216.
16. Mormon 9:7-8.

These gifts, according to the context of the passage in the Book of Mormon, were to continue while the world stands-- except for unbelief.

Numerous examples of Mormons speaking in tongues are to be found in their literature. Some twenty persons spoke in tongues at the dedication of the Kirtland temple. Brigham Young talked in what Joseph Smith called the "true Adamic language." The gift of tongues acquired status in the church, and although Joseph Smith continued to warn of its misuse, it became one of the most popular "gifts of the Spirit." Fife writes concerning attitude of the Mormon toward the gift:

> *From the beginning of Mormonism down to the present day the gift of tongues and the power of interpretation thereof has been taken as a manifestation of the highest degree of heavenly inspiration of which a human being is capable.*[17]

As late as 1919 the president of the Mormon church devoted an entire sermon to substantiation of the gift of tongues during the general conference. Tongue-speaking is still very much a part of Mormonism.

It should be noted that "tongue speaking" and "latter-day revelations"are supported on the same premise within Mormonism. To accept one would be to accept the other. To deny one would be to deny the other. This presents a knotty problem to the glossolalist today who can not accept the Book of Mormon. If he accepts the "tongue-speaking" gift of the Mormons, he must accept the revelation with which it is connected. If he denies the Book of Mormon being latter-day revelation from God, then he must deny the "tongue-speaking" gift connected

---

17. Austin and Alta Fife, Saints of Sage and Saddle (Indiana University Press, 1956), p. 230.

with it. It is logically impossible to accept the sign if one denies the content of the revelation.

Mormonism and the Campbell movement arose in the same cultural milieu. The two movements differed sharply on authority. Campbell's movement held to the objective--once for all--authority of the Scriptures. The Mormon movement held to the subjective continuing revelation as also constituting authority.

In the Campbell movement, those individuals and churches which accepted "an experiential faith" based on visions, tongue speaking and feeling followed Sidney Rigdon into Mormonism. It is but a short step from an "experiential faith" based on subjective experiences into the acceptance of latter-day revelations like the Book of Mormon.

Those within churches of Christ who might consider the glossolalia experience a thing to be desired would do well to learn this lesson from history. Those who refuse to learn from history are destined to repeat it.

SECTION III

TEXTUAL EVIDENCE

The New Testament evidence must be the center of any discussion of glossolalia. To determine if glossolalia is from God or men, one must go to the only external objective evidence available from God--the Scriptures.

It is not a question of "What God is able to do." It is not a question of "How one chooses to interpret abnormal unexplainable psychological experiences." The question is "What does the Bible say?"

To discover religious practices approved of God one does not begin with the traditions or experiences of men and then find proof passages. He must first go to the New Testament and then make his practices conform to it. To discover spiritual truth about God, one does not begin with his own judgment and then go to the New Testament to find supporting passages. He must first go to the New Testament to discover spiritual truth and make his judgment conform to it. The New Testament must always be the only source of determining religious practice and spiritual truth. It is wrong for man's own experience and/or judgment to be the primary source and the New Testament the secondary source.

There are two questions that these four chapters will endeavor to answer: (1) Does the New Testament teach that the gift of speaking in tongues was to be a continuing gift in the church throughout all ages? (2) Is the glossolalia phenomenon experienced in our time the *glossa* gift of the New Testament? To answer these questions each of the New Testament texts dealing with the gift of speaking in tongues will be discussed.

CHAPTER 7

MARK 16:17-20

Jesus mentioned speaking in tongues only one time in the Gospel record. It was connected with the giving of the great commission according to Mark. The context of the passage tells how tongues and other signs would follow them that believe. Following the promise of the signs which will accompany them that believe, Mark gives a commentary and says that the promise was fulfilled in the preaching of the apostles. Verses seventeen and eighteen contain the promise:

And these signs shall accompany them that believe: in my name shall they cast out demons; they shall speak with new tongues; they shall take up serpents, and if they drink any deadly thing, it shall in no wise hurt them; they shall lay hands on the sick, and they shall recover.

A Problem of the Text

The first question to ask in the study of a passage concerns the genuineness of the text. That is, does the passage itself belong in the canon of Scripture? Is it from apostolic and inspired men or is it a later gloss placed in the text by uninspired men? Textual scholars have validated all but a very few of the New Testament passages through detailed critical studies. It just happens that the ending of Mark--verses 9-20--is one of those passages which is still questioned as belonging to the gospel of Mark.

The English translations demonstrate this textual problem. The King James Version includes the passage without notation.

The American Standard Version adds a footnote on the passage stating: *"The two oldest Greek manuscripts, and some other authorities, omit from verse 9 to the end. Some other authorities have a different ending to the Gospel."*

The Revised Standard Version does not include the passage in the text, but places it in a footnote. The New English Version places both this passage along with an alternate ending to the Gospel of Mark in the text. The Today's English Version also places the two different endings in the text.

This confusion among the translators is caused by manuscripts not agreeing as to the correct ending of Mark. The two oldest unical manuscripts--the Siniaticus and the Vaticanus—do not contain these verses. There is, however, a blank space at the end of Mark in these manuscripts which indicates that the scribes knew something was missing. The passage does have the support of the unical manuscripts Alexandrinus, Bezae, Ephraemi Rescriptus and Washingtonianous. Added to these, the passage has the support of all late unicals, all cursives and most of the ancient versions. It is significant that the Peshitta Syriac, Old Italic, Sahidic and the Coptic versions contain the passage. The textual evidence is about equally divided on whether or not to include the passage.

Whatever one might decide about the genuineness of this passage, it is evident that it is from the first century. Irenaeus quoted it. Both Tatian's Diatessaron and probably Justin Martyr accepted it as a part of Mark. There is good textual evidence for its inclusion at the end of the Gospel of Mark. Even if the passage should not be included at the end of Mark, it still must be dealt with as a first-century reference of the gift of tongues. It is uncritical to ignore this passage because of certain textual problems connected with it. This author accepts the passage as belonging to the Gospel of Mark.

Commentaries offer little assistance on this passage. The one thing that most standard commentaries have in common concerning this passage is the way little or no attention is given to it. McGarvey is typical. His only comment is:

> *The book of Acts gives examples of each one of these signs except the fourth, and though we have no record of a disciple escaping the effects of drinking poison, there is little doubt that in many persecutions such cases did occur.*[1]

Books dealing with tongue speaking often pass over the passage lightly. Phillips does not discuss it in his thesis on The Meaning of Glossa in the New Testament.[2] Walker passes over it lightly by saying, "The passage in St. Mark is itself involved in many uncertainties to be a reliable witness in this investigation."[3] Even if one questions the genuineness of the passage in the New Testament, it still must be dealt with as a historical witness.

The passage is one of the proof texts of glossolalists and can not be ignored. It is important as a reference to tongue speaking from the mouth of Jesus. It is important in determining the purpose of the gift.

Jesus promised in the passage that believers would have signs to confirm the gospel that the apostles were to preach. Jesus worked miracles to show that he was from God,[4] but there is no record that he ever spoke in tongues. He did promise that this would be one of the gifts exercised by those to

1. J. W. McGarvey, The Fourfold Gospel (Cincinnati: The Standard Publishing Co., n.d.), pp. 763-64.
2. Paul Phillips, The Meaning of Glossa in the New Testament (an unpublished M. A. Thesis at Abilene Christian College, 1963).
3. Dawson Walker, The Gift of Tongues (Edinburgh: T&T Clark, 1906), p. 6.
4. John 3:2; 20:31.

whom the apostles preached. The apostles understood that the tongue speaking on the day of Pentecost and at the household of Cornelius was a fulfillment of the promise that Jesus made of being baptized in the Holy Spirit.[5]

Who Shall Work Signs?

A second question about this passage is: "Who are the ones who will work these signs?" The passage says that *"these signs shall accompany them that believe,"* but what believers does it have reference to? Does it refer to the apostles only, those who received gifts by the laying on of the apostles' hands, or to believers in all ages?

The broad context of the passage is talking about the disbelief of the apostles. They disbelieved the report of Mary Magdalene. They disbelieved the report of the two who saw the Lord in the way.[6] Jesus upbraided them because of their unbelief.[7] Perhaps the passage means that the apostles would have signs following them after they turned from their unbelief. Acts tells of many miraculous signs done by the apostles. They cast out demons and healed the sick.[8] They spoke in new tongues.[9] Mark's comments after the promise of Jesus also fits this interpretation: *"And they went forth, and preached everywhere, the Lord working with them, and confirming the word by the sign that followed."*[10] Such an interpretation of the passage is very appealing, but it does not fit all of the facts.

A close look at the passage shows a change from indirect

5. Acts 11:15-17.
6. Mark 16:11-13.
7. Mark 16:14.
8. Acts 19:11-12.
9. Acts 2:4.
10. Mark 16:20.

discourse to direct discourse. This grammatical change makes such an interpretation impossible. This can be illustrated by italicizing the direct discourse in the passage. Since the direct discourse of the passage are the words of Jesus, they are set off in red in the red-letter editions of the New Testament:

> ... And he upbraided them with their unbelief and hardness of heart, because they believed not them that had seen him after he was risen. 15. And he said unto them, *Go ye into all the world, and preach the gospel to the whole creation. 16. He that believeth and is baptized shall be saved; but he that disbelieveth shall be condemned. 17. And these signs shall accomapny them that believe: in my name shall they cast out demons; they shall speak with new tongues; 18. they shall take up serpents, and if they drink any deadly thing, it shall in no wise hurt them; they shall lay hands on the sick, and they shall recover.* 19. So then the Lord Jesus, after he had spoken unto them, was received up into heaven . . . .

In the verses preceding this passage Mark tells of the resurrection appearance of Jesus--this is indirect discourse. In verse fifteen Jesus gives the great commission to the apostles. He said, *"Go ye."* This begins the direct discourse. In verse sixteen Jesus is still talking, but he is not speaking of the apostles. He said, *"He that believeth . . . . "* In verse seventeen Jesus is still talking about *"He that believeth . . . . "* When Jesus promises *"these signs shall accompany them that believe,"* he is still talking about *"He that believeth . . . . "* He uses the third person. If he were referring to the apostles he would have used the second person, *"ye"* as he did in verse fifteen.

In the direct discourse of verses fifteen through eighteen Jesus is speaking directly to his apostles. When the first person is used, Jesus is referring to himself, *"in my name shall they cast out demons."* When the second person is used Jesus refers to the apostles, *"Go ye . . . . "* When the third person is used Jesus is referring to *"He that believeth and is baptized."*

Beginning with verse nineteen, the passage changes back to indirect discourse. Mark comments about the promises being fulfilled in the ministry of the apostles.[11]

Those who believe and are baptized are the ones who will have signs accompanying them. Does this not mean then that such signs will accompany anyone who believes and is baptized today? If it did, then every baptized believer would be able to work signs. Common sense observations tell us that this is not the case. It took more than being a baptized believer to possess the gifts of the Spirit in the New Testament accounts. Certainly it is not different today.

Luke's account of the conversion of the Samaritans illustrates this point.[12] Philip the evangelist came to Samaria when the church was scattered because of persecution. He preached Christ to the people of Samaria and worked signs. Philip had already received the laying on of the apostles' hands.[13] Many Samaritans believed and were baptized. A sorcerer by the name of Simon was also baptized. Now if the promise of Jesus in Mark 16:17-18 was made only on the conditions of faith and baptism, the Samaritans would possess the gifts of healing, tongues, casting out demons, etc. But they did not. Luke records:

> *Now when the apostles that were at Jerusalem heard that Samaria had received the word of God, they sent unto them Peter and John: who when they were come down, prayed for them, that they might receive the Holy Spirit for as yet it was fallen upon none of them: only they had been baptized into the name of the Lord Jesus. Then laid they their hands on them and they received*

11. Roy Lanier, "Mark 16:17-18," Firm Foundation (August 18, 1970), p. 521.
12. Acts 8:4-24.
13. Acts 6:6

the Holy Spirit.[14]

Baptized believers they were, but possessors of the Holy Spirit they were not.[15] The apostles had to lay hands on them before they could receive him. Philip, who had already received the laying on of the apostles' hands, could work these signs promised by Jesus. Those who had only believed and been baptized could not. The difference was in "the laying on of the apostles' hands." This is made very clear in verse eighteen. The passage gives the reaction of Simon when he saw what the apostles were doing by laying their hands on the Christians in Samaria:

Now when Simon saw that through the laying on of the apostles' hands the Holy Spirit was given, he offered them money, saying, Give me also this power that on whomsoever I lay my hands, he may receive the Holy Spirit.[16]

Simon saw that the Holy Spirit could be given only by apostles. It was not enough to be a baptized believer, the apostles also had to lay on their hands.

This same principle is shown in other places. After Paul baptized the twelve disciples of John the Baptist in Ephesus, he laid hands on them. After the laying on of hands by Paul, an apostle, they began to speak in tongues.[17] Paul is probably speaking of this apostolic power of bestowing gifts in his letter to Timothy. He says, *"For which cause I put thee in remembrance that thou stir up the gift of God, which is in thee*

14. Acts 8:14-17.
15. The Samaritans had received the gift of the Holy Spirit promised to all who repent and are baptized (Acts 2:38), but not the power of the Holy Spirit that came by the laying on of apostles' hands. The Holy Spirit is the same in both cases but His work in the individual is different.
16. Acts 8:18-19.
17. Acts 19:7.

through the laying on of my hands . . . . "18

The interpretation of the passage now becomes clear. The signs of new tongues, casting out demons, taking up serpents, etc., are to accompany baptized believers who have received the laying on of the apostles' hands. This understanding is necessary. The text itself shows that baptized believers are meant. Other passages in the New Testament show that being a baptized believer alone is not sufficient to receive the gifts. Such powers were conveyed to baptized believers through the laying on of the apostles' hands.

The Purpose of Signs

The third question that must be answered in this passage concerns the purpose of these signs. Why did God give these signs of drinking poison without injury, picking up snakes without harm, healing the sick, casting out demons and speaking in new tongues? Were they to make the recipients feel more spiritual? Were they to be proof of salvation and God's approval? Were they to be exhibited before mass meetings to stir people into religious revival?

The passage itself speaks clearly about the purpose. Mark says that the apostles preached and the Lord worked with them *"confirming the word by the signs that followed . . . . "19* The purpose of the signs was to confirm the word that the apostles preached.[20] Jesus gave the promise. Mark said that it was fulfilled.

The validation of the gospel message was demonstrated by signs. God, by these signs, was showing that those who gave

18. II Timothy 1:6.
19. Mark 16:20.
20. II Corinthians 12:12.

the message were his messengers. New revelation has always been accompanied by signs. This was true when Moses received the law from Sinai. There was tempest, darkness and the burning with fire. There was the sound of a trumpet and the voice of words.[21] These signs were given in order that the people would not refuse Him that spoke from heaven. Signs accompanied the new revelation of the law. Signs also accompanied the messages of the Old Testament prophets. Daniel was spared in the lion's den. Elijah and Elisha worked wonders before the people to confirm the message they spoke. When God has a new revelation for man, he always confirms it with signs.

The revelation of God in Jesus Christ was confirmed with signs. John speaks of this. *"Many other signs therefore did Jesus in the presence of the disciples, which are not written in this book: but these are written that ye may believe that Jesus is the Christ, the Son of God."*[22] Nicodemus understood this when he said to Jesus, *"Rabbi, we know that thou art a teacher come from God; for no one can do these signs that thou doest, except God be with him."*[23]

A passage in the book of Hebrews shows this same principle --God confirms his word with signs:

Therefore we ought to give the more earnest heed to the things that were heard . . . which having at the first been spoken through the Lord, was confirmed unto us by them that heard; God also bearing witness with them, both by signs and wonders, and by manifold powers, and by gifts of the Holy Spirit.[24]

The message first spoken by Jesus and delivered to us by

21. Hebrews 12:18ff.
22. John 20:30f.
23. John 3:2.
24. Hebrews 2:1-4.

apostles was confirmed with signs. This was the promise of Jesus in Mark. This was fulfilled in the ministry of the apostles. The new revelation that the apostles preached needed confirmation with signs from heaven.

Signs have always accompanied new revelation. If there is no new revelation, there is no need for signs. If there is new revelation which the signs confirm, the revelation of Jesus is incomplete and the Scriptures are not sufficient. This is the point of danger in the glossolalia doctrine today. Signs mean new revelation. New revelation means that Jesus and the Scriptures are inadequate.

Five kinds of signs are mentioned in the text . . .casting out demons, speaking in new tongues, taking up serpents, drinking deadly poison and healing the sick. If any one of these signs were to continue, then all of them would. One claiming the signs of "new tongues" today must also affirm the signs of "taking up serpents" and "drinking deadly poison." Proof for one is proof for the other. A question for contemporary glossolalists is this: Since it is a common practice to have meetings for exercising the "gift of new tongues" why are there not also meetings to exercise the gift of "drinking deadly poison?"

Mark 16:14-20 is an important passage in understanding the gift of tongues in the New Testament. Although it contains certain textual problems, it must be considered in any discussion of New Testament evidence on the *glossa* gift. The passage shows that tongue speaking was a promise by Jesus himself. The promise was given to baptized believers who received the laying on of the hands of the apostles. The purpose of the gift-- along with the others mentioned in the passage--was to confirm the word--Gospel--as it was spoken by the apostles and those who received the laying on of the apostles' hands.

CHAPTER 8

THE GLOSSOLALIA GIFT IN ACTS

Acts 2:1-13

The most positive description of speaking in tongues is given by Luke in Acts 2. This was the first occurrence of the phenomenon which was promised by Jesus and later practiced in Ceasarea, Ephesus and Corinth. Four questions should be answered about the *glossa* gift at Jerusalem on the day of Pentecost: (1) Who spoke in tongues? (2) What was the nature of the tongues? (3) How were the tongues received? (4) What was the purpose of the tongues?

Twelve apostles spoke in other tongues on the day of Pentecost. There were 120 of the brethren present at the choosing of Matthias to take the place of Judas.[1] A large multitude of people gathered together after the apostles began to speak in other tongues. But it was only the twelve who received the gift. Three things point to this conclusion:

First, only the apostles received the promise of the baptism of the Holy Spirit. Luke tells how Jesus was with his apostles before his ascension and tells them:

> *"John indeed baptized with water; but ye shall be baptized in the Holy Spirit not many days hence ... But ye shall receive power when the Holy Spirit is come upon you and ye shall be my witnesses ..."*[2]

The baptism of the Holy Spirit was promised only to the ap-

1. Acts 1:15ft.
2. Acts 1:5, 8.

promised only to the apostles--not to the 120.

Second, the immediate context would infer that the twelve apostles were meant, Luke says, *"They were all filled with the Holy Spirit, and began to speak in other tongues."* In the Greek there is no pronoun, "they." The subject of the verb "were filled" is "all" . . . *pantes*. *Pantes* is used to refer to the whole company of the 120 in verse fourteen; to the multitude who came together in verses seven and twelve; to the twelve apostles in verse thirty-two; and to all of the believers in Jerusalem in verse forty-four. To discover which of these is meant in verses 1-4, one must see which fits the immediate context. The last group identified in the context is the "eleven apostles" in 1:26. Beginning with verse five a new group is identified--"devout men from every nation." From this it would seem that "all"--*pantes*--in. verses one, two and four refers to the twelve apostles. J. W. McGarvey writes:

> *This is made certain by the grammatical connection between the first verse of this chapter and the last of the preceding. Taken together they read as follows: "And they gave lots for them, and the lot fell upon Matthias and he was numbered with the eleven apostles. And when the day of Pentecost was now come, they were all together in one place."*[3]

It was Matthias and the other eleven apostles who received the Holy Spirit and spoke in other tongues.

Third, references to those speaking in tongues best fit the apostles. Those speaking in tongues were Galilaeans. So were the apostles. To still the rumor of drunkenness on the part of those speaking in tongues, Peter stood up with the eleven.[4]

3. J. W. McGarvey, New Commentary on Acts of Apostles (Des Moines, Iowa: Eugene S. Smith, 1892), p. 21.
4. Acts 2:14.

The audience's response to Peter's sermon was addressed to *"Peter and the rest of the apostles."*[5] The apostles were special witnesses of the resurrection. This was one of their qualifications.[6] Those who witnessed Jesus' ressurection are the ones mentioned in connection with the pouring forth of the extraordinary things which the people heard and saw on the day of Pentecost.[7]

Only the twelve apostles received the baptism of the Holy Spirit on the day of Pentecost. This fulfilled the promise of the baptism of the Holy Spirit made by Jesus and confirmed them as witnesses of the resurrection. They alone spoke in tongues. The baptism of the Holy Spirit was not for the 120, nor for the multitude. Neither was tongue speaking given to any but the apostles on that day. The tongue-speaking gift was connected with the baptism of the Holy Spirit. It was another physical sign like the sound of a rushing of a mighty wind and cloven tongues like as fire.

The nature of the gift of tongues on the day of Pentecost has already been discussed.[8] Luke understands "speaking in other tongues" to mean "speaking in other languages." All of the evidence within the context points to this conclusion.

Pentecost was the first manifestation of "tongues." Luke is the only New Testament writer to give a full description. Following Luke one should regard all other New Testament references to the *glossa* gift as one speaking in other languages unless otherwise identified. All of the references to "tongues" in Acts must be identified with the language gift on the day of Pentecost.

5. Acts 2:37.
6. Acts 1:22.
7. Acts 2:32-33.
8. See page 36 ff.

The *glossa* gift in I Corinthians is connected to events of Pentecost through Isaiah 28:11: *"Nay, but by men of strange lips and with another tongue will he speak to this people . . . . Yet they would not hear."*[9] Paul quotes this passage in I Corinthians 14:21. Peter used the same terms for "other tongues" as was used in the Isaiah passage in the Septuagint. Isaiah uses *glosses heteras* and Peter used *heterais glossais.*

Walker shows that attempts that have been made to discredit the view that the *glossa* gift of the New Testament was language arises from a rejection of Luke's credibility. He writes:

> *Modern critics are, for the most part, at one in approaching the consideration of Pentecost from the standpoint of St. Paul's information in I Corinthians. They differ considerably in the resulting view of the credibility of St. Luke's narrative as entirely fictitious, to the more orthodox and cautious, which is inclined to suspect that St. Luke's story gives an amplified and perhaps slightly distorted version of the original event.*[10]

The credibility of Luke has been more firmly established in the twentieth century through the work of such men as William Ramsey.[11] If one accepts the miraculous events of the New Testament, he should have no problem in accepting Luke's account of the miraculous speaking in other languages on Pentecost.

The gift of tongues on the day of Pentecost was received through the baptism of the Holy Spirit. Jesus had promised such a baptism.[12] Peter explained the things the people saw

---

9. Isaiah 28:11-12.
10. Dawson Walker, The Gift of Tongues (Edinburgh: T&T Clark, 1906), p. 21.
11. William Mitchell Ramsay, St. Paul the Traveler and Roman Citizen (New York: G. P. Putnam's Sons, 1896),
12. Acts 1:5, 8.

and heard as being that which was sent by Jesus through the Holy Spirit. He says: *"and having received of the Father the promise of the Holy Spirit, he hath poured forth this, which ye see and hear.*[13]

Later at the household of Cornelius, Peter could look back on the events at Pentecost and say:

> *And as I began to speak, the Holy Spirit fell on them, even as on us at the beginning. And I remembered the word of the Lord, how he said, John indeed baptized with water; but ye shall be baptized in the Holy Spirit.*[14]

Peter understood the events on both Pentecost and at the household of Cornelius to be the results of the baptism of the Holy Spirit. The promise of Jesus was fulfilled.[15]

At Ephesus the gift of tongues was not given through the baptism of the Holy Spirit. This baptism was only received on those two memorable occasions when the Jews and Gentiles first had the gospel preached to them.

The baptism of the Holy Spirit and the accompanying phenomenon of speaking in tongues could hardly be identified with the work of the Holy Spirit in a believer's baptism. Paul said, *"In one Spirit were all baptized into one body"* and were *"all made to drink of one Spirit."*[17] All of the Corinthians were baptized in one Spirit and were made to drink of one Spirit but it is clear that not nearly all spoke in tongues.[18]

13. Acts 2:33.
14. Acts 11:15-16.
15. Acts 2:4; 10:46.
16. Acts 19:6.
17. I Corinthians 12:13.
18. I Corinthians 12:30.

This should make it clear that the baptism of the Holy Spirit on the day of Pentecost was not to be received by all.[19]

The purpose of the gift of tongues in the New Testament has already been shown.   To these one might add two special purposes on Pentecost.

First, a special purpose of the *glossa* gift on Pentecost was to give an external sign of the fulfillment of Jesus' promise to baptize with the Holy Spirit. It, along with the visible "tongues like as fire" and the audible "speaking in other tongues," showed that the apostles had received the baptism of the Holy Spirit.[20]

Second, another special purpose of the *glossa* gift on Pentecost was to fulfill the prophecy of Joel. Peter quotes Joel 2: 28-32 and says that it was fulfilled by the gift of tongues on Pentecost: *". . . this is that which hath been spoken through the prophet Joel: and it shall be in the last days, saith God, I will pour forth my spirit upon all flesh . . . ."*[21] The Joel passage does not mention "speaking in tongues." It mentions dreams, visions, prophesying and signs in heaven and earth, but not tongue speaking. Peter sees the fulfillment of Joel's prophecy in the pouring forth of God's Spirit which was audibly manifested to the crowd in the speaking in other tongues. It was in this way that Joel's prophecy was fulfilled.

Acts 10:44-48

There are two other incidents of speaking in tongues in Acts. Neither is described in detail since Luke has already explained

19. R. L. Roberts, "A Note on I Corinthians 12:13", Restoration Quarterly. II, (1st Quarter, 1958), pp. 45-47.

20. Acts 2:33.

21. Acts 2:16-17.

the gift in Acts 2.

The second incident of tongue speaking is found in Acts 10: 44-48. The *glossa* gift came upon those who had gathered at the household of Cornelius while they were listening to the preaching of Peter. Luke writes:

> *While Peter yet spake these words, the Holy Spirit fell on all them that heard the word. And they of the circumcision that believed were amazed . . . because that on the Gentiles also was poured out the gift of the Holy Spirit. For they heard them speak with tongues, and magnify God.*[22]

Three things stand out in this incident of tongue speaking.

First, the Gentiles received the baptism of the Holy Spirit as well as the Jews on the day of Pentecost. This is made even more clear when Peter reports the conversion of the Gentiles to the brethren in Jerusalem. He said: *"The Holy Spirit fell on them, even as on us at the beginning."*[23] It may be significant that Luke records three incidents of speaking in tongues in the book of Acts. (1) On Pentecost when the Jews first received the gospel; (2) At the household of Cornelius when the Gentiles first received the gospel; (3) At Ephesus when the disciples of John first heard the gospel from Paul.

Second, the purpose of the gift of tongues at the household of Cornelius was to show the Jewish brethren who had come with Peter that the Gentiles could also be saved. Peter was going to be criticized for going into the house of a Gentile. Some of the Jewish brethren were critical of preaching the gospel to those outside of the Jewish nation. Because the Gentiles were able to speak in tongues, Peter could reply to his critics: *"If*

22. Acts 10:44-46.
23. Acts 11:15.

then God gave unto them the like gift as he did also unto us when we believed on the Lord Jesus Christ, who was I, that I could withstand God?"[24]

Third, the household of Cornelius spoke in tongues before they were baptized into Christ. It was their receiving the gift of tongues that prompted Peter to ask, *"Can any man forbid water, that these should not be baptized?"* This passage shows that the gift of tongues was a sign which had nothing to do with salvation,[25] spirituality or the gift of the Holy Spirit received at baptism.[26] It was rather a sign to convince people of some truth that God was revealing for the first time.

Acts 19:1-6

The third incident of tongue speaking is found in Acts 19:6. On this occasion, the *glossa* gift came upon twelve men--former followers of John the Baptist--after they had been baptized received the laying on of Paul's hands. Luke writes:

> *And when they heard this, they were baptized into the name of the Lord Jesus. And when Paul had laid his hands upon them, the Holy Spirit came on them; and they spake with tongues, and prophesied.*

This incident is different from the other two since they were able to speak in tongues because Paul--an apostle--laid his hands on them. There is no indication that they received the baptism of the Holy Spirit as they did on Pentecost and at Cornelius' house. The means of receiving the *glossa* gift is different here from the other two incidents in Acts.

24. Acts 11:17.
25. Mark 16:16.
26. Acts 2:38.
27. Acts 19:6-7.

CHAPTER 9

THE GLOSSA GIFT AT CORINTH

In Mark there is the promise of tongues from Jesus. In Acts, Luke records tongue speaking on the great occasions of Jews, Gentiles and the followers of John the Baptist coming into the kingdom. In I Corinthians there are problems connected with speaking in tongues that Paul must correct.

Mark points out the purpose of tongue speaking as one of the signs to confirm revelation. Luke describes the nature of tongue speaking and shows how the gift was received. Paul corrects men who are making a mockery of a God-given gift. One cannot understand the New Testament *glossa* gift by isolating one passage from the other. All three apostolic men write of the *glossa* gift from a different perspective. One must take all of the evidence together to understand tongue speaking in the New Testament.

There is no evidence that the *glossa* gift at Corinth was any different from that on Pentecost. As will be shown, the Corinthians were abusing the real *glossa* gift and perhaps letting pagans come into the assembly and counterfeiting it.

These two factors made things look a lot differently at Corinth than they had at Jerusalem, Ceasarea and Ephesus. The *glossa* gift was the same however. It was its abuse and counterfeit that made the difference. Any differences in its manifestation can be explained as difference existing between its right use and its abuse. It has already been shown that the evidence indicates that the *glossa* gift was the same in all of the New Testament passages.

The Corinthian Christians were abusing the divine gift.[1] Its proper use brought edification. Its improper use brought confusion. Possessing a divine gift did not necessarily mean spiritual maturity. Neither did it guarantee right conduct. The prophet Balaam had the Spirit of God but his character and conduct were evil.[2] Peter possessed great powers from the Spirit, but it did not keep him from showing prejudice at Antioch. In Galatians 2 Paul had to rebuke him to his face.

Paul sees the problem of tongue speaking at Corinth as threefold. Each of the three chapters deals with one aspect of the tongue-speaking problem. (1) The *glossa* gift was a showy gift and those who possessed it felt above the other Christians who did not have it. Paul refutes this concept in chapter twelve. (2) The possessors of the *glossa* gift make it the apex of their Christian experience. In chapter thirteen Paul shows that such gifts without love are worthless. (3) The exercise of the *glossa* gift caused confusion in the assembly. In chapter fourteen the apostle shows that the purpose of these spiritual gifts was edification and lays down rules for exercising them.

It is not surprising that problems over the use of spiritual gifts arose at Corinth. The religious background of the Corinthian Christians had diverse roots. Some were Jews and were accustomed to the quiet synagogue worship. They were used to sitting in silence listening to the reading of Scripture and joining in the singing of Psalms. The women sat apart in the synagogue and never led in the religious exercises. Some of the Corinthian Christians were former pagans. They had been accustomed to the wild, frenzy religious celebrations of the

1. It should be noted that even though the gift was divine the exercise of it was subject to the human will. See I Corinthians 14:32. Paul could criticize the way they were abusing the gift without criticizing the Holy Spirit who gave it.
2. Numbers 22-24.

mystery religions. Women played a prominent role in many of their emotionally-charged religious practices. Baird gives a graphic description of some of the cults of Corinth. He suggests that the practices of these cults must be seen in the background of the worship confusion in the church at Corinth. He writes:

> *Those who came out of Hellenistic religions, on the other hand, were familiar with other kinds of thirst. Devotees of Dionysus, the god of intoxication, were given to bacchanalia--wild orgastic feasts where food and wine were devoured in quantity. Some of these rites were faintly reminiscent of more primitive ritual in which enthusiasts, mostly women, whipped themselves into a frenzy, leaped upon a hapless animal, tore him limb from limb and drank the blood, still warm and living. Although the Hellenistic age had softened much of this savage sort of worship, some of the old practices--frenzied revels, sensualism, and self-castration--still continued. Greco-Roman religion was no more bloodless than its precursors. The cult of Mithras, which was so popular with the Roman troops, initiated its converts in the taurobolium--a pit in the ground over which a bull was slaughtered. As the blood poured over him, the new devotee eagerly let it immerse his eyes, nose, and tongue. This sort of thing makes it pretty clear that many of the Corinthians would not be satisfied with silent prayer.* [3]

Christians who had participated in such emotional, irrational and frenzy ceremonies would be apt to abuse the supernatural gifts received from the Spirit. The *glossa* gift was by its very nature most likely to be abused. It caused the possessor to speak in another language that he did not understand. This would certainly be stimulating. Since others who did not know the language could not understand it, it made the possessor of the gift somebody special. When a number of these

3. William Baird, The Corinthian Church (New York: Abingdon Press 1964), pp. 120-21.

who had the *glossa* gift all began speaking at the same time, frenzy was caused similar to that which was experienced in the mystery religions. This was impressive to those who craved emotional religious excitement.

I Corinthians 12

The main teaching of chapter twelve is that possession of spiritual gifts--including the *glossa* gift--does not make one better than other members of the body. Every member of the body is mutually dependent upon every other member of the body. No member--even those without these extraordinary gifts--was unimportant. Neither were those members who possessed showy supernatural gifts above the other members of the body. They could not say, *"I have no need of thee."* 4 The supernatural gifts possessed by the Christians at Corinth were from the one Spirit and were for the edifying of the one body. There was no just cause for the possessors of these gifts to glory.

The first verses of the chapter lay down a basic principle that the Corinthians needed to learn about the worship experience: One cannot always trust his own feelings. Paul writes:

> *Now concerning spiritual gifts, brethren, I would not have you ignorant. Ye know that when ye were Gentiles ye were led away unto those dumb idols, howsoever ye might be led.* 5

When the Corinthians were still idol worshippers, they had emotional experiences in their worship. Paganism aroused men's feelings. The mystery rites were very stirring. None could deny it. When they became Christians, they came to understand that pagan worship was wrong. Even though

4. I Corinthians 12:21,22.
5. I Corinthians 12:1-2.

paganism stirred their emotions and aroused their "religious feelings," it was erroneous. This very experience should teach them that their emotions were not dependable as religious authority. Captivated by religious feeling, pagans worship dumb idols. Under the influence of arousing rituals, pagans are led into all kinds of irrational practices. As has already been shown, ecstatic utterance was one such practice.[6] Paul wanted the Corinthians to understand this principle at the outset of his discussion. One cannot trust his feelings in religion.

Suppose a Christian at Corinth possessed the *glossa* gift. He liked to use it even though he and others could not interpret. He particularly liked to use it in company with others who were exercising the *glossa* gift. Everyone talking in a strange language at one time charged the air with excitement. It stirred him up. It excited his religious feelings. He felt he was really a spiritual man because of this feeling. Paul corrected such a man. He reminded him that such excitement of religious feelings was common in paganism and certainly did not indicate superior spirituality.

Paul posed another practical problem. How is one going to determine whether his religious experience is inspired by the Holy Spirit or if it is mere enthusiasm excited by rousing rituals like those used in dumb idol worship? All religions have practices which stir the emotions and which give satisfying experiences to its advocates. How can one tell if these experiences are from God or merely the counterfeits of the devil? Paul answers: *"Wherefore I make known unto you that no speaking in the Spirit of God saith, Jesus is anathema; and no man can say, Jesus is Lord, but in the Holy Spirit."*[7] The criteria is the confession of the Lordship of Jesus. This is the way to determine if the one "speaking in the Spirit" is

6. See page 42-45, 59-61.
7. I Corinthians 12:3-4.

doing so through pagan enthusiasm or inspiration of the Holy Spirit.

The Scriptures often warn Christians to beware of the deceitful workings of the devil under the guise of religion. Paul warns the Galatians of those who would preach a perverted gospel. They were not to receive it even though its advocates might claim to have received it from an angel of heaven.[8] Paul warned the church at Thessalonica about the "man of sin." His coming was *"according to the working of Satan with all power and signs and lying wonders, and with all deceit of unrighteousness for them that perish."*[9]   Jesus warns of false Christs and false prophets who will *"show great signs and wonders, so as to lead astray, if possible even the elect."*[10] John warns in Revelations of sign workers from the devil whose purpose was to deceive those who dwell on the earth.[11] In his first epistle John says, *"Believe not every spirit, but prove the spirits, whether they are of God; because many false prophets are gone out into the world."*[12] There were messengers of the devil at Corinth who were trying to deceive people under the guise of religion. He mentions them in another letter:

> For such men are false apostles, deceitful workers, fashioning themselves into apostles of Christ. And no marvel; for even Satan fashioneth himself into an angel of light. It is no great thing therefore if his ministers also fashion themselves as ministers of righteousness.[13]

The *glossa* gift from the Holy Spirit at Corinth was the ability to speak in a foreign language. There is the possibility

8. Galatians 1:6-10.
9. II Thessalonians 2:9-10.
10. Matthew 24:24.
11. Revelation 13:13-14; 16:13-14.
12. I John 4:1.
13. II Corinthians 11:13-15.

that false apostles and deceitful workers of the devil were counterfeiting the gift. They could use the same ecstatic utterances that were used in the worship of dumb idols and claim to be "speaking in the spirit." The Corinthians were abusing the real *glossa* gift by all speaking in the assembly at one time and without the aid of an interpreter. It would be easy for these deceitful workers to go undetected in such a situation. Perhaps this is the reason Paul gives this criteria for separating the real from the counterfeit "speaking in the spirit." He did not want a messenger of Satan in the Corinthians assembly cursing Jesus. He instructs the Corinthians that an interpreter must be present on all occasions. By means of the translator, one could know if a person were praising or cursing Jesus.

This passage in 12:3-4 presents a problem to the glossolalist today. If in their "speaking in the spirit" neither they nor any man knows what is being said, how can they be sure they are praising Christ instead of cursing Christ? They have abandoned their will and reason to what they believe to be the Holy Spirit. But is it the Holy Spirit or is it an unholy spirit of the devil? How can they know if their utterance is praising or cursing? There is no understanding of what is said to determine which it is? Are they going to let such an important thing as this be determined by mere feelings? This is the same criteria that the Gentiles had when they were led away unto dumb idols.

There are two lists of spiritual gifts in chapter twelve.[14] The first lists gives nine gifts that come from the Spirit: (1) word of wisdom, (2) word of knowledge, (3) faith, (4) gifts of healing, (5) working of miracles, (6) prophecy, (7) discerning of spirits, (8) kinds of tongues, (9) interpretation of tongues.

14. I Corinthians 12:8-10; 28-30.

The apostle listed these as examples of the diversity of the gifts. The point is that no matter how diverse the gift, the source is the same-- the Spirit.

If the Holy Spirit be the source of all of these gifts, then there should be no individual pride in the person possessing any one of them. The possession of any one of the gifts did not make one member of the body any more spiritual than any other member of the body. It was not because of their merit that they received the gift; it was because God so willed it.[15] The same Spirit gives different gifts to different members to be used for the good of the whole body.

It should be noted that Paul did not understand the *glossa* gift as being ecstatic utterances coming from man's psyche. The *glossa* gift was not from demons which produced vain babblings in the pagan cults. The source of the *glossa* gift was the Holy Spirit. The source of the counterfeit gift which called Jesus anathema was from an unholy spirit. The real *glossa* gift was just as supernatural as the working of miracles and the gifts of healing. This refutes tne interpretation that *"misguided teachers at Corinth simply spoke in languages they had learned, but in languages unknown by the average member."*[16] The supernatural is involved in these gifts. If the *glossa* gift were no more than languages learned by natural means, then it does not belong in a listing of supernatural gifts. If the *glossa* gift were no more than estatic utterances, there was nothing which would make it distinct from the pagan practices. But Paul said that the *glossa* gift was from the Holy Spirit.

The second list of spiritual gifts in the chapter also includes nine gifts. This list varies from the original list by excluding

---

15. I Corinthians 12:18.
16. Paul V. Dobson, "The Key to Tongues," Firm Foundation (January 27, 1970), p. 52.

four of the first list and including four new gifts. These nine are: (1) apostles, (2) prophets, (3) teachers, (4) miracles, (5) gifts of healings, (6) helps, (7) governments, (8) kinds of tongues, and (9) interpretation.

It should be noted that "kinds of tongues" and "interpretation of tongues" are given last in both lists. Paul himself says there are "greater gifts"[17] and *"greater is he that prophesieth than he that speaketh with tongues."*[18] Perhaps they are placed at the bottom of the list because they were the least of the gifts of the Spirit. Paul would not say that the *glossa* gift was unimportant. He told the Corinthians to *"Forbid not to speak with tongues,"*[19] and *"desire earnestly spiritual gifts."*[20] Every member of the body is important. Every gift of the Spirit exercised by every member of the body in Corinth was important and needed.[21]

Among the spiritual gifts, however, prophecy is better than tongues. This teaching of Paul would certainly have a humbling effect on those who were so proud of their showy gift of tongues in Corinth. The *glossa* gift did not make them super Christians. They found that they possessed the least edifying, most abused, and often useless gift of the Spirit. Paul put it at the bottom of the list.

Spiritual gifts were not signs of personal glory. Paul is plain about this. He said that *"to each one is given the manifestation of the Spirit to profit withal."* [22] It is God who set the gifts in the church[23] *"even as it pleased him."*[24] Gifts did not

17. I Corinthians 12:31.
18. I Corinthians 14:5.
19. I Corinthians 14:39.
20. I Corinthians 14:1.
21. I Corinthians 12:21.
22. I Corinthians 12:7.
23. I Corinthians 12:28.
24. I Corinthians 12:18.

come because of individualistic merit. They are gifts of God. Neither were they a sign of maturity or spirituality. Sayers writes:

> *It is worthy of observation that the charismatic gifts make nobody a more mature Christian, produced no real growth of any sizable significance, never purified the heart of the person or the church, did not save anybody nor guarantee anybody personal salvation . . . .*[25]

The *glossa* gift in chapter twelve is listed last among the other spiritual gifts from the Spirit. Possessors of spiritual gifts should have understood that the gifts were given to them, not because of personal glory, but for building up the church. Paul also warns against letting the exercise of spiritual gifts become like the excitement of the pagan cults which also claimed to be god-possessed.

I Corinthians 13

Chapter thirteen is Paul's response to those who thought the *glossa* gift was the apex of Christian experience. John McRay writes:

> *In the 13th chapter Paul wanted the Corinthians to understand that, rather than making them the spiritually elite, the possession of these gifts was in fact no guarantee of their-favor with God or spiritual maturity.*[26]

The thirteenth chapter is introduced by the last verse of chapter twelve: *"And moreover a most excellent way show I unto you."* Paul shows that there is something better for the spiritual development of the Corinthian church than these spiritual gifts. He points them to the way of love.

The first problem of chapter thirteen is the phrase *"tongues*

25. Stanley E. Sayers, "Religion Experience Verses Spiritual Maturity" (unpublished paper, 1970), p. 1.

26. John McRay, "Spiritual Gifts in First Century Worship" Integrity (January, 1972), p. 110.

of men and of angels." It is easy to see that the "tongues of men" refer to languages. But to what do the "tongues of angels" refer? Some have regarded this as the language that angels speak. Such an interpretation betrays an ignorance of the nature of angels. Angels are spirits.[26] A spirit does not have flesh and bones.[27] How could angels have languages when they do not possess flesh and bones to form the words? "Tongues of angels" can not refer to physical tongues of an-

Barnes suggests that "tongues of angels" could have reference to "unspeakable words, which it is not lawful for a man to utter" that Paul heard when he was caught up to the third heaven.[28] The passage itself does not allow such an interpretation. The words Paul heard in the third heaven were "unspeakable" while the tongues of 13:1 are speakable. It is impossible to prove conclusively just what is meant by the phrase because it is not explained in the New Testament. Walker offers the most attractive interpretation. He says that the phrase can *"best be regarded as the rhetorical amplification of the simpler genē glōssōn (tongues of men)."*[29] Perhaps the "tongues of angels" can best be regarded as a hyperbole.[30]

Paul makes an inspired prediction in 13:8, *"whether there be tongues, they shall cease."* This must have come as quite a shock to those who gloried in the *glossa* gift at Corinth. He had just told them that they became as sounding brass or a clanging cymbal when they exercised their gift without love. Now he tells them that their *glossa* gift was going to cease. Paul also said that the other supernatural gifts of prophecies and knowledge were also to be done away. Tongues seem to be particularly emphasized. Prophecies and knowledge "shall be

27. Luke 24:39; Hebrews 1:14.

28. Albert Barnes, Notes, Explanatory and Practical, on the First Epistle of Paul to the Corinthians (New York: Harper Brothers, 1870), p. 260.

29. Dawson Walker, op. cit., p. 9.

30. James D. Bales, Pat Boone and the Gift of Tongues (Searcy, Arkansas: James D. Bales, 1970), p. 77ff

done away," but tongues "shall cease." If the *glossa* gift was going to cease while other things remain, it surely could not be as important as some of the Corinthian Christians believed. Paul did not even include it along with prophecy and knowledge as a part of the "perfect." He said:

> For we know in part, and we prophesy in part; but when that which is perfect is come, that which is in part shall be done away.[31]

Nothing is said about speaking in tongues "in part". He previously said they were to cease of themselves. Miraculous knowledge and prophecy which were incomplete--only partial gifts--were to be replaced by "that which is perfect." Tongues did not need replacement. They had served their purpose and were to cease of themselves--without replacement.

The coming of the "perfect"was the time when these miraculous gifts were to become inoperative. What is the "perfect?" When was it to come? These questions are not easily answered. The Corinthians must have known what was meant by "perfect," but its meaning has been difficult to grasp in later times. Different authors have interpreted "perfect" to mean (1) the coming of Christ in judgment, (2) the perfect state of heaven, (3) the body or the church, (4) love, the abiding gift, and (5) the full revelation of God's word.[32]

The word translated "perfect" is *teleion*. It is in the nominative case, singular number, and in the neuter gender.

31. I Corinthians 13:9-10.
32. Numerous articles have appeared on the interpretation of **to teleion** since the first printing of this book. Three are particularly significant. John McRay, **"To Teleion in I Corinthians 13:10"** Restoration Quarterly, (3rd and 4th Quarter, 1971), pp. 168-183. Leroy Garrett, John McRay, Roy Osborne, Jim Reymolds, Rubel Shelley and Carl Spain, "That Which is Perfect" Christian Chronicle, (June 5, 1972), pp. 1-15. Gary Workman, Has That Which is Perfect Come? (4000 W. Oakey Blvd., Las Vegas, Nevada: Gary Workman, 1971).

Arndt-Gingrich gives the definition as being "having attained the end or purpose, complete, perfect. He also suggests that the term can sometimes mean mature, full-grown and fully developed. R. L. Roberts brings together a number of authors in his study of the word:

> *Thayer has:* 'Brought to its end, finished: wanting nothing necessary to completeness; perfect;' Moulton-Milligan: 'literally having reached its end; hence, full-grown, mature . . . in good working order . . . complete, final.' It also might be well to point out Trench's contribution: 'The various applications of teleion are all referable to the telos, which is its ground.' The meaning of telos is given as: '1. end: most frequ. of the termination or limit of an act or state (in NT also of the end of a period of time, cl. teleute),' In accordance with these facts Lenski very aptly says that 'when the complete shall come' refers to the 'goal in comparison with what is still on the way.' If so, whatever 'the perfect' means, it must be the goal, the completion, the perfecting of something yet unfinished, undeveloped, imperfect or 'on the way.'[33]

Whatever meaning is given to the word must carry with it the idea of "complete, mature or finished."

Some have understood "the perfect" to refer to the second coming of Christ. T. C. Wisenbaker writes: "Evidently when that which is perfect comes, when we see face to face and when we understand fully can only refer to the time of the second coming of Christ."[34] This interpretation has two problems: (1) Faith, hope and love are to abide even when "the perfect" has been realized. When Christ comes, faith will be made sight, and hope will find fulfillment. The perfect can

33. R. L. Roberts, "That Which is Perfect'—I Corinthians 13:10" Restoration Quarterly, (4th Quarter, 1959), pp. 201-02.
34. T. G. Wisenbaker, "The Work of the Holy Spirit Today" (unpublished paper, n.d.), p. 1.

not then refer to the coming of Christ. (2) Roberts shows that the grammar can not allow this interpretation. He writes,

The fact that it is in the neuter gender makes it clear that it could not possibly be in reference to Christ, for it would then have to be masucline in gender.[35]

Barnes is among those who have suggested "the perfect" to refer to future life in heaven.[36] This interpretation still has the same problem given in (1) above. The coming of "the perfect" is at a time when faith, hope and love still exist. Faith and hope will have given away to sight and fulfillment in heaven. Paul said, *"Hope that is seen is not hope."*[37] Faith is *"a conviction of things not seen."*[38]

J. W. McGarvey takes the view that "the perfect" refers to the second coming of Christ and the perfect state of the Christian in heaven. Unlike Wisenbaker, he contends that the miraculous gifts have ceased and only the effects or fruits of knowledge and prophecies will continue until that which is perfect has come. He writes:

But if the gifts have passed from the church as transient and ephemeral, shall not that which they have produced abide? Assuredly they shall, until that which is perfect is come; i. e., until the coming of Christ. Then prophecy shall be merged unto fulfillment, and the dim light of revelation shall be broadened into the perfect day. We today see the reflection of truth, rather than the truth itself. It has come to us through the medium of minds which, though divinely illuminated, were yet finite, and it has modified itself though essentially spiritual, so as to be clothed in earthly words; and it is grasped and comprehended by us through the use of our material brains.

35. R. L. Roberts, loc. cit.
36. Albert Barnes, op. cit., p. 271.
37. Romans 8:25.
38. Hebrews 11:1.

Thus, though perfect after its kind, and true as far as it goes, our present knowledge of heavenly things is perhaps as far from the full reality as is the child's conception of earthly things.[39]

McGarvey's interpretation has some things to commend it. Heaven is certainly viewed by a Christian as being a "perfect state" in which dark things will be made clear and knowledge will become complete. This interpretation still has the same problems as listed in (1) and (2) above. Faith and hope are earthly attributes. They are not needed in heaven. Grammar will not allow "the perfect" to be Christ. To these two objections Roberts adds another:

It is important that we notice that the phrases 'in part' modified 'knowledge' and 'prophecy' as miraculous gifts. It can not be made to modify anything else here. Some have expressed the view that the reference here is to knowledge and prophecy as the effects of the spiritual gifts. They agree that the gifts have passed away, but their effect, i. e., revealed truth, will continue until we have perfect knowledge in heaven. But, what is there in the text to show that the effect of the gifts and not the gifts themselves is meant? The apostle does not have under consideration the effects of the gifts, but the gifts themselves.[40]

A unique interpretation of "the perfect" came to the attention of this author through a bulletin article.[41] Wayne Jackson reviewed a paper presented at the Hartford Forum in December, 1969, in which Paul Logue of St. Louis contended that "the perfect" referred to the church. Since chapter twelve speaks of the body, the church, he believes this same

39. J. W. McGarvey, Thessalonians, Corinthians, Galatians and Romans (Cincinnati: The Standard Publishing Co., 1916), p. 132.
40. R. L. Roberts, loc. cit.
41. Wayne Jackson, "Tongues," The Christian Courier (Stockton, California: East Main Street Church of Christ, n.d.), p. 23.

thought is carried over into chapter thirteen. He reasons that when the church is perfected or matured, then the gifts would cease. He further suggests that since the church is still immature (carnal minded) gifts are still needed and must remain. Since *sōma* (body) is neuter, this would fit the gender of *teleion* (perfect). This interpretation is very strained. Certainly the neuter *sōma* agrees with the neuter *teleion*, but so do scores of other New Testament words. To try to make "perfect" agrees with "the body" of chapter twelve, one must go back through discussions of many things. The cessation of gifts, the importance of love and a listing of spiritual gifts are all discussed before one gets to the body discussion of chapter twelve. There is nothing in the context of 13:10 to merit such a hermeneutical leap. It seems odd that a glossolalist would come up with this interpretation. Such an interpretation would infer that those who claim "tongue speaking" today are immature and carnal minded while those who do not practice "tongue speaking" are mature and perfected. This is not the usual claim of a glossolalist.

"Love" has sometimes been given as the correct interpretation of "the perfect." Jack McKinney writes:

The Greek word for "perfect" bears besides its absolute sense also the meanings 'complete' and 'mature' (cf 14: 20, where it is translated 'men'). We must note too that in the original, to see 'face to face' means no more in its figurative use than seeing 'clearly' or 'fully.' There is nothing in this context which would indicate that Paul is thinking of the end of time and Christ's return. 'That which is perfect' is none other than love, the subject of the entire chapter. Nor must any object, 'But love in this age is not perfect.' In Paul's discussion, when compared to miraculously imparted and spiritually external charismata, love is perfect, conceptually. It is the very goal of all Christian growth and service. It is that inner, mature, complete, spiritual grace which unites all other virtues in itself (vs. 4-7). It is in fact in Paul's mind 'the bond of perfectness' (Col. 3:14). In I Corinthians 13 Paul has progressed through the various grace-gifts toward the same goal as in Ephesians 4:7-16: maturity in love. What he is saying to the Corinthians however, who even in the use of spiritual gifts are behaving childishly and carnally, is: Come now, it is time to start putting away our blocks and grow up.[42]

Such an interpretation has much to commend it. The subject of "love" is the context in which "the perfect" is found. Love is shown to be the mature and enduring gift and is contrasted to the immature and passing spiritual gifts. This interpretation fits Paul's other statements in Ephesians 4:9-16 and Colossians 3:14. There are two major problems with this interpretation.

First, the gender of *teleion* is neuter and the gender of *agape* is feminine. If Paul meant "the perfect" to be "love" certainly he would have used *teleia* instead of *teleion*. The adjective must agree with the noun it modifies.

Second, the immediate context of "the perfect" refers to the passing of the spiritual gifts of knowledge and prophecy. Notice the passage with words capitalized for emphasis:

For we know IN PART, and we prophesy IN PART; but when that which is perfect is come, THAT WHICH IS IN PART shall be done away . . . now I know IN PART; but then shall I know fully even as also I was fully known.[43]

"The perfect" and the "in part" are in contrast. That which is "in part" is but a segment of that which is "perfect." "The perfect" must be understood in terms of that which is "in part." The miraculous gifts of knowledge and prophecies are what

42. Jack McKinney, "The Cessation of Supernatural Spiritual Gifts" (unpublished paper, November 14, 1970), pp. 2-3.
43. I Corinthians 13:9.

Paul considers to be "in part," therefore that which is "perfect" must be the completion of or the maturing of these gifts. Love has no part in this discussion of the passing of spiritual gifts. Love is the broad context. The passing of spiritual gifts is the immediate context which is tied together by the contrast of "that which is perfect" and "that which is in part."

A common interpretation of "the perfect" is that it refers to the complete revelation of God's word in the Scriptures. Roberts writes:

> The early church was dependent upon oral revelation by holy apostles and prophets for its knowledge of the will of God. God placed the message in inspired men . . . . enabling them to speak as the Holy Spirit gave them utterance. Thus, the word of God was revealed--in part-- gradually, until it was 'once for all delivered unto the saints' (Jude vs. 3), and written by inspiration as a full revelation of the Divine word.[44]

Problems exist in the passage which are difficult to solve with this or any other interpretation. This interpretation has been objected to for four reasons.

First, glossolalists generally object to this interpretation because it refutes their practice of "tongue speaking." If "the perfect" refers to the complete revelation of God in the Scriptures which has been completed, there could be no authority for glossolalia today. The gifts were to pass when the perfect (completed revelation of God in the Scriptures) has come, so the gifts have passed away. This objection is based upon an attempt to read a present religious practice into the text of the Scriptures.

Second, some have objected to this interpretation because

44. R. L. Roberts, op. cit., p. 199.

they believe that Paul did not intend to prove the passing of the miraculous gifts in this passage. Charles Melton presents this view:

> *Though the idea that spiritual gifts would cease long before the coming of Christ is true to Scripture, it is questionable that the Corinthians would have felt that Paul was endeavoring to prove that point . . . . It is likewise doubtful that the Corinthians ever imagined that Paul was proving a threefold division of time into 1) an age of gifts, 2) an age of cessation of gifts but continuance of faith and hope, and 3) an age of eternal love. It is not that this division is not true, only that they would more naturally have understood him to be saying that love is to control God's people whatever and whenever it might be. (It also could be pointed out that if Paul was endeavoring to prove that gifts were to cease that more positive language could be used.) The arguments used in support of an age of church maturity are, for the most part good. The only question is whether the age of complete revelation is under discussion in this passage.*[45]

Melton points out the obvious. Paul's primary purpose in the passage was not to prove that the Scriptures were to cause the spiritual gifts to cease. His purpose was to show that faith, hope and love were superior to the gifts of prophecies, tongues and knowledge. The spiritual gifts were temporary and were to cease when "that which is perfect is come." Faith, hope and love will still abide. Whatever the purpose of Paul's statement, the passage is true. It can be used to teach other things not even under discussion. God's word is always true.

The truth Paul spoke to a certain problem in his day can be used with equal force for a problem in the twentieth century.

45. Charles Melton, "Perfect in First Corinthians Thirteen" (unpublished paper presented in Pepperdine College, December 13, 1965), pp. 5-6.

One so far removed from Paul in time and circumstances cannot know all of the motives he had in writing a passage. He cannot fully know all of the things the Corinthians had in mind when they received the passage. All one has is the words of the Scriptures. They are sufficient to apply in every situation for all time.

The third objection comes as a reaction to the use of James 1:25 to prove that the "perfect" of I Corinthians 13:10 is the perfect law of liberty. This is a valid objection. James writes, *"But he that looketh into the perfect law, the law of liberty . . . . "* To say that because James used "perfect" in this way means that Paul meant the "perfect law of liberty" in I Corinthians is not good exegesis.

Fourth, a more serious objection to this interpretation is that "prophecies" and "knowledge" do not agree in gender with "perfect" in this passage. Both prophecies *propheteia* and knowledge *gnosis* are feminine while perfect *teleion* is neuter. This would indicate that "the perfect" included more or something different from a fullness of knowledge and complete prophecies. This presents a problem. It has already been shown that miraculous porphecies and knowledge were "a part" of the "perfect."[46] If knowledge and prophecies are a part of "the perfect" but are not to be identified with it because of the difference in gender, what can "the perfect" be?

It has been suggested that it could be "the holy scriptures" *ta hiera grammata. Grammata* is neuter, but one has to go to II Timothy 3:15 to find it. It certainly is not in the context of I Corinthians 13.

Perhaps a better guess would be "gift." The Greek word is *charisma;* It is neuter in gender. The word is in the context.

46. See page 118.

In both lists of spiritual gifts in chapter twelve, the word is used repeatedly. It is so much a part of the context that the translators have inserted italicized *"gifts"* in 13:2 and 14:1. In the immediate context of "the perfect" prophecies, tongues, and knowledge are discussed. All of these are called gifts, *charismata* in other places.

If *charisma*--"gift"--is considered the antecedent to "the perfect," how would it fit into the context? Perhaps very well. The apostles show that the temporary spiritual gifts, that tongues, prophecies and knowledge were to cease. But why? Because there is coming "the perfect (gift?)" which will make all of them unnecessary. If *charisma*--"gift"--is the correct antecedent, the question of "the perfect" is still unsolved. The problem has been changed from "what is 'the perfect?' " to "what is 'the perfect gift?' " The full revelation of God in the Scriptures still appears to be the best answer.[47] The Scriptures are a gift of God to man.[48] They are complete and in this sense, perfect. They are the only thing that makes all of the miraculous spiritual gifts unnecessary. With them signs are unnecessary.[49] With them the gifts of prophecies and knowledge are unnecessary.[50] Study of the Scriptures produces Christian maturity that makes the administrative gifts of the Spirit unnecessary.

In spite of these objections, it appears that the best interpretation of the perfect" is "the full revelation of the Divine Word." None of the objections are insurmountable.[51]

This interpretation can be illustrated in three steps. (1) The

47. If "the perfect" is charisma then this would remove one of the objections to the interpretation of "love" on page 122f.
48. II Peter 1:21.
49. John 20:31.
50. II Timothy 3:16-17.
51. Hebrews 5:14.

miraculous gifts of prophecies and knowledge were to be done away--become inoperative. (vs. 8) (2) The miraculous gifts of prophecies and knowledge are only in part--only a segment of the whole. (vs. 9) (3) When the perfect--of which prophecies and knowledge are but a part--is come, these gifts, along with the other spiritual gifts, will become inoperative. (vs. 10)

These gifts were to cease because they were incomplete. In verse nine, the Greek particle *gar* is used. It is translated "for." *Gar* is often employed in Greek when giving a reason or explanation. This is what Paul is saying. Prophecies and knowledge were to be done away and tongues were to cease because--*gar*-- they were only "in part." When the perfect came there was no further need for them.[52]

It should be observed that the gift of tongues is not discussed by Paul as a part of "the perfect." He only deals with the gifts of prophecies and knowledge. A different verb is used with the other two gifts. Tongues, it appears, are placed at the bottom of the list again. They are not said to even be a part of "the perfect." They were to cease of themselves, unlike the gifts of prophecy and knowledge that would become inoperative because of the coming of "the perfect."

I Corinthians 14

The fourteenth chapter is a discussion of the gifts of tongues and of prophecy. It may be divided into four sections: (1) The gift of prophecy is better than the gift of tongues (vss. 1-12). (2) The importance of interpretation (vss. 13-19). (3) Tongues are a sign to the unbelieving (vss. 20-25). (4) Directions for keeping down confusion in the assembly when the gifts of tongues and prophecy are being used (vss. 26-40).

52. R. L. Roberts, op. cit., p. 200.

It has already been shown that the *glossa* gift in I Corinthians 12-14 referred to foreign languages instead of ecstatic utterances.[53] The glossolalia adherents today do not find support in this chapter. The *glossa* gift of the Corinthians had ceased of itself.

Paul begins the chapter by saying that prophecy is preferred before tongues. This is the discussion of the first twelve verses.

In verses 1-4, he says that tongue speaking is from God back to God. The speaker does not understand. The hearers do not understand. The only possible good that it does is that the speaker in some way is edified by the experience. Paul sees in these verses a case in which the one who speaks in the foreign language is unlearned himself and is speaking to others who are unlearned in the language. No interpreter is present to give the translation.

In verses 5-6, Paul says that the one who prophesies is greater than the one who speaks in tongues. The one who prophesies edifies the church. This must have been a hard saying for those at Corinth who felt superior because of their *glossa* gift. Paul adds that if the one who spoke in tongues also translated the language, he could also edify the church.

In verses 7-10, an illustration is given. Paul says that tongue speaking cannot edify unless it is understood. Just as the sounds of a harp or pipe can not produce music unless it is understood. Sound without meaning to the hearer is like speaking into the air. Tongue speaking in the church is a colossal waste of words.

In verse 11 the apostle shows that the glossa gift created barriers rather than promoted understanding. It made brothers in the church seem like barbarians. Paul concluded in

53. See page 35-45.

verse twelve, *"since ye are zealous of spiritual gifts, seek that ye may abound unto the edifying of the church."*

Three basic things should be noted in this section: (1) Tongue speaking of itself is unedifying to the church. (2) The one who speaks in tongues, instead of being superior, is really inferior to the one who prophesies. Prophesying builds the church, tongue speaking builds the ego. (3) Tongue speaking alienates because it makes barbarians of brothers.

The second section of chapter fourteen deals with the importance of interpretation. The section begins with Paul saying, *"Wherefore let him that speaketh in a tongue pray that he may interpret."*[54] The one speaking in tongues is to interpret for two reasons. First, the interpretation is for his own understanding (vs. 14). Second, the interpretation allows the unlearned to say "amen." (vs. 16)

In verses 14-15, the apostle shows the importance of both the spirit and the understanding being active in prayer and praise. When one prays in a tongue, his understanding is unfruitful. The one praying should pray with both the spirit and the understanding. The one singing should sing with both the spirit and the understanding. No worship takes place when the will and mind is passive. If the words coming from the mouth are "as the Spirit give utterance" instead of "out of the abundance of the heart," the mind and will of man is passive. The words come from God and are directed to God; man is made a passive thing. Worship can no more take place in such a situation than it can by a tape recorder in an empty church building. God wants heart worship. He wants the understanding to be fruitful.

The passage contradicts the present teaching of the

54. I Corinthians 14:13.

glossolalists who say that tongue speaking should be sought for the experience rather than the content. Such a view is expressed by Martin:

" *Its value, therefore, was not to be found in its message—content, but rather in its demonstrative quality in its supposed ability to make manifest the fact of the indwelling Spirit.* "[55]

Paul says just the opposite. The Corinthians were to understand what they were saying in the praise and prayers. Tongue speaking is not some private devotional language. At Corinth those who possessed the *glossa* gift were to pray that they might interpret so their own understanding would not be unfruitful. Not only is the speech of the contemporary glossolalists different from the possessors of the *glossa* gift at Corinth, but often the very purpose of the present phenomenon is in opposition to the New Testament gift.

One should beware of surrendering his will to an experience. He might think he is surrendering it to the Holy Spirit when in reality it could be an unholy spirit. The devil is able to counterfeit the work of God that is revealed in the Scriptures. He is able to fill a person's heart as he did Ananias' when he lied to the Holy Spirit.[56] He is able to snatch the Gospel out of the heart of one who hears it.[57] Man must always maintain control of his own will. God wants his followers to be able to will, to reason and to understand his relationship with them. When one surrenders his reason and will, he gives up that which makes him distinctive as man. It is only by reason and will that one is able to discern truth from error and practice righteousness instead of sin. To abandon these for an experience is dangerous.

55. Ira J. Martin, "The Place and Significance of Glossolalia in the New Testament Church" (unpublished Doctor's Dissertation, Boston University, 1942), p. 111.

56. Acts 5:3.

57. Matthew 13:19.

In verses 16-17 Paul shows the second important reason to interpret tongues. Only by an interpretation can others be edified. When you give thanks in another language, one who is unlearned in that language cannot give his "amen" to it. It might have been a prayer of thanksgiving or it might have been pronouncement of cursing. He does not know.

Public worship is not a monologue—God talking to himself through the mouth of a man. Neither is it a dialogue—man talking to God without regard to others in the assembly. It is rather a trilogue—man talking to God from his heart and being understood by other men who can say "amen." Public worship must touch three corners of a triangle—God, me and my brother. It must be pleasing to God. It must be from both my spirit and my understanding. It must be edifying to my brother. None of these can be neglected in worship. To neglect any one makes worship inadequate.

Paul possessed the *glossa* gift. He spoke in tongues more than any of the Corinthian Christians. There is a record of Paul speaking in Greek and Hebrew.[58] Being a Roman citizen, he could well have known Latin also.[59] Besides these, Paul no doubt possessed the gift to speak in many other languages. Yet, he said that he would rather speak five words of understanding than ten thousand words in a foreign language. When he spoke, he wanted people to understand.

The third section of chapter fourteen shows that tongues are a sign to the unbelieving. He begins the section by exhorting the Corinthians to grow up—be mature. The way some at Corinth were using the *glossa* gift, one would think they were children in understanding. They acted like a five-year-old child playing cowboy and Indian with a loaded pistol. Some at Corinth did not see the real significance of the *glossa* gift.

58. Acts 21:37; 22:2.
59. Acts 22:25-28.

They were playing with it as if it were a toy. Paul tells them to grow up and be men.

To show that tongues are a sign to the unbelieving, Paul uses three things. (1) A quotation from the Old Testament. (2) A statement of the significance of the *glossa* gift. (3) An illustration from their experience in the assembly.

A difficult problem exists in this passage. Who are the "unbelievers?" One would normally identify the "unbelievers" as being pagans. It is so used throughout I Corinthians.[60] Even in this passage the "unlearned or unbelieving" of verses 23 and 24 refer to pagan outsiders.

> *If therefore the whole church be assembled together and all speak with tongues and there come in men unlearned or unbelieving, will they not say that ye are mad? But if all prophesy, and there come in one unbelieving or unlearned, he will be reproved of all . . . .*[61]

The "unbelievers" here must be pagan outsiders. The whole church is assembled. These "unbelievers" come in from outside the assembly. The passage clearly shows that they were observers rather than participants.

Verse 22 says that *"tongues are for a sign . . . to the unbelieving."* It is difficult to make the "unbelieving" in verse 22 fit the "unbelieving" of verses 23-24. In verse 22 tongues are a sign to the "unbelieving." In verse 23 tongues are thought to be madness by the "unbelieving."

Further complicating the identity of the "unbelieving" is the quotation from Isaiah 28. The Old Testament passage clearly identifies the ones to whom foreign languages became a

60. I Corinthians 6:6; 7:12; 13, 14, 15, 10:27.
61. I Corinthians 14:23-24 a.

sign. They were Jews—God's people. They were not pagan outsiders.

These problems force one to seek another explanation for the "unbelieving" in verse 22. Such an explanation can be found in a comparison between Isaiah 28 and Paul's use of it in this passage. God's people in Isaiah's time rejected prophecy. In this sense they were unbelieving. God's people at Corinth in Paul's time rejected prophecy and preferred tongues. In this sense they were unbelieving. Other New Testament passages show the possibility of God's people becoming unbelieving. The father of the epileptic boy had enough faith for Jesus to heal his son, but he still cried, *"I believe: help thou mine unbelief."*[62] Many of God's people died in the wilderness before they got to the land of Canaan because of "unbelief."[63] Christians—God's people—are exhorted in Hebrews 3:12: *"Take heed, brethren, lest haply there shall be in any one of you an evil heart of unbelief, in falling away from the living God."*

New Testament writers did not always quote from the Old Testament in context. They often used a passage to show something entirely different from its original meaning. Matthew's quotation of Hosea 11:1 is an example. Hosea was referring to Israel while Matthew was referring to Jesus when he said, *"Out of Egypt did I call my son."* Sometimes, however, one cannot understand a New Testament passage until he has seen the context of the Old Testament passage which is quoted. This is true of Paul's quotation from Isaiah 28.

To understand this passage one must first study the context of Isaiah 28. It would be well to open a Bible to Isaiah 28 and I Corinthians 14:20-25 and read the verses.

62. Mark 9:24.
63. Hebrews 3:19.

First, look at 14:20-25. This passage can be outlined in the following way.

Verse 20 contains a practical exhortation to grow up and be men. This exhortation comes after Paul has written at length on the value and purpose of spiritual gifts. He is particularly critical of the immature way they are using the *glossa* gift. He says, *"Brethren, be not children in mind: yet in malice be ye babes, but in mind be men."*

Verse 21 is a quotation from Isaiah 28:11-12. Paul uses the Old Testament authority to back up his exhortation and lays the foundation for his statement that *"tongues are for a sign . . . to the unbelieving."* The Isaiah passage is particularly significant here because it fits the Corinthian situation. Both rejected plain prophecy. Both were to hear foreign languages as a sign of their unbelief.

> *In the law it is written, by men of strange tongues and by the lips of strangers will I speak unto this people; and not even thus will they hear me, saith the Lord.*[64]

Notice the Isaiah passage is talking about the people of God— the Jews. Paul also is talking to the people of God at Corinth. He calls them "brethren" in verse 20.

Hodge gives an excellent explanation of this passage:

> *He does not quote the passage as having any prophetic reference to the events in Corinth . . . . It is a simple reference to a signal event in the Jewish history from which the Corinthians might derive a useful lesson. The Jews had refused to hear the prophets speaking their own language, and God threatened to bring upon them a people whose language they could not understand. This was*

---

64. I Corinthians 14:21.

> *a judgment; a mark of displeasure designed as a punish-*
> *ment and not for their conversation.   From this the*
> *Corinthians might learn that it was no mark of divine*
> *favor to have teachers whose languages they could not*
> *understand.   They were turning a blessing into a curse.* [65]

Verse 22 contains Paul's interpretation of the Isaiah passage. His interpretation fits the Corinthian situation. The Corinthian Christians like the hearers of Isaiah did not want to hear the clear teaching of the Lord.   They refused to hear plain prophecy, then they must hear tongues as a sign of their unbelief.

> *Wherefore tongues are for a sign, not to them that be-*
> *lieve, but to the unbelieving: but prophesying is for a*
> *sign, not to the unbelieving, but to them that believe.''*

The "unbelieving" in this passage must not be understood as pagan unbelievers. Tongues were not to be a sign to them. The "unbelieving" of verse 22 is to be distinguished from the outsider who is "unlearned or unbelieving" in verse 23ff. The "unbelieving" of verse 22 are the people of God who refuse to hear plain prophecy. It was God's people in Isaiah's day who refused to hear. It was God's people or Christians who refused to hear at Corinth. John McRay writes:

> *Tongues were also a sign for the unbeliever who will be*
> *forced to receive the message of God in a foreign lan-*
> *guage, since he rejects God's teaching in his own lan-*
> *guage.* [66]

Verses 23-25 were a contemporary illustration used by Paul to show that tongues were a sign to the unbelieving. Tongues

65. Charles Hodge, An Exposition of the First Epistle to the Corinthians (Grand Rapids: Wm. B. Eerdmans Publishing Co., 1959), p. 293.

66. John McRay, "Spiritual Gifts in the First Century" Integrity (January, 1972), p. 110.

were not a sign to the believer; they preferred plain prophecy. They did not need signs. Tongues were not a sign to the "unlearned or unbelieving" outsider. They would have considered talking in a foreign language which neither they nor anyone else understood sheer madness. The only ones left are the unbelieving people of God who refused to hear plain prophecy. The tongue sign was not a sign of God's favor. It was a sign of God's disfavor because they rejected plain prophecy. Paul deals sharply with those who were abusing the *glossa* gift at Corinth. They thought they were the spiritual elite and under God's special favor. Paul told them that tongues could also be a sign of God's disfavor.

> *If therefore the whole church be assembled together and all speak with tongues, and there come in men unlearned or unbelieving, will they not say that ye are mad? But if all prophesy, and there come in one unbelieving or unlearned, he is reproved by all, he is judged by all; the secrets of his heart are made manifest; and he will fall down on his face and worship God, declaring that God is among you indeed.*[67]

This certainly shows that "tongue speaking" is not a tool of evangelism. It also shows that "tongue speaking" is not for the spiritually strong believers; they prefer prophecy. At Corinth, tongue speaking was for the immature Christian who in unbelief preferred the *glossa* gift to plain edifying prophecy.

An understanding of the context of Isaiah 28:11-12 confirms this interpretation. Isaiah had predicted God's judgment upon Jerusalem from Assyria. The rulers refused to hear the word of the Lord. Isaiah said to them:

> *Wherefore hear the word of Jehovah, ye scoffers, that rule this people that is in Jerusalem. Because ye have*

67. I Corinthians 14:23-25.

*said, We have made a covenant with death, and with
Sheol are we at agreement; when the overflowing scourge
shall pass through, it shall not come unto us; for we have
made lies our refuge, and under falsehood have we hid
ourselves . . . . (but God said) your covenant with death
shall be annulled, and your agreement with Sheol shall
not stand; when the overflowing scourge shall pass
through, then ye shall be trodden down by it.*[68]

The covenant they made with Egypt was a covenant of death
and would not stand.   Assyria would pass through like a
scourge and they would be trodden down.

Instead of hearing the plain prophecy of the Lord from
Isaiah, the rulers of Jerusalem listened to the arrogant and dis-
solute priests and prophets.   Isaiah describes them:

*And even these reel with wine and stagger with strong
drink; the priest and the prophet reel with strong drink,
they are swallowed up of wine, they stagger with strong
drink; they err in vision, they stumble in judgment.*[69]

His description is graphic.   Priests and prophets were trying to
conjure up a vision by human means.   They used drugs—wine
and strong drink.   They succeeded in getting a vision and an
experience.   It was not from God.   The vision was false and the
experience was the reeling and staggering of a drunk person.
They accepted it and convinced the rulers that it was a genuine
message from God.   He who wants a vision strong enough will
find a way to get one—even if it is not from God.   The priests
and the prophets illustrate this point.   He who wants to
believe a message will find a way to do so—even if it is a lie.
The rulers illustrate this point.

The priests and the prophets did not like Isaiah.   He spoke

68. Isaiah 28:14-15, 18.
69. Isaiah 28:7-8.

the plain prophecy of God. They spoke false visions brought on by wine. The two could not agree. The priest and the prophets responded to the prophetic oracle Isaiah pronounced in verses 1-6. They asked a rhetorical question: "Will he teach us knowledge?" They suggested that the only one who would hear Isaiah's message would be young children and little babies. They thought they had nothing to learn from Isaiah's pronouncement.

In verse 10 they take up a jibe against Isaiah, *"Caw laqaw, caw laqaw,"* they cry. This jibe has been translated many ways. The ASV's wording is *"For it is precept upon precept, precept upon precept; line upon line, line upon line; here a little, there a little."* Some Hebrew scholars understand these phrases to be non-translatable gibberish. Others think it refers to the language of children or even the mutterings of a drunk man.[70] Even if the translation is not clear, the meaning is understood. The priests and the prophets thought they knew how to direct their own ways by methods of their own devising. They did not need the message of Isaiah. They regarded his pronouncements as words in the wind, not to be taken seriously.

Verses 11-13 are the verses quoted in part by Paul. It is the reply of Isaiah to the jibes of the priests and the prophets:

Nay, but by men of strange lips and with another tongue will he speak to this people; to whom he said, This is the rest, give ye rest to him that is weary; and this is the refreshing: yet they would not hear, Therefore shall the word of Jehovah be unto them precept upon precept, precept upon precept; line upon line, line upon line; here a little there a little; that they may go, and fall backward, and be broken, and snared, and taken.

70. R. B. Y. Soctt, "The Book of Isaiah," The Interpreter's Bible Editor, George A. Butterick, Vol. V (New York: Abingdon Press, 1956). p. 316.

Since they would not hear the plain prophecy of Isaiah, they would hear God's message of judgment from men of another language. This referred to the Assyrians who would soon be in their streets as conquerors. They refused to hear the word of the Lord and considered it as words in the wind, not to be taken seriously. They soon would hear it from the lips of foreigners. Rejection of the word of the Lord would cause them to be broken.

Hodge gives the meaning of the passage:

> . . . . *The meaning is, that when a people are disobedient, God sends them teachers whom they can not understand; when they are obedient, he sends them prophets speaking their own language. This is the natural conclusion from the premises contained in verse 21. When the Hebrews were disobedient God sent foreigners among them; when obedient, he sent them prophets. Wherefore, i.e. hence it follows, that unintelligible teachers are for the unbelieving; those who can be understood are for the believing.*[71]

Notice the following comparisons between the priests and the prophets of Isaiah and those who abused spiritual gifts in Corinth.

(1) The priests and the prophets believed the the word of the Lord pronounced by Isaiah was too simple and babyish for them (v. 9.) The Corinthians felt that prophecy in plain language was too simple for them; they needed the mysterious utterances of tongue speaking (14:2).

(2) The priests and the prophets did not take the pronouncement of Isaiah seriously (vs. 9-10). It was meaningless

71. Hodge, op. cit., p. 296.

words. In its place they devised by their own judgment—a confused and erring vision brought on by intoxication (vs. 7-8). The Corinthians did not take the words that came by prophecy seriously but sought the will of the Lord via tongue speaking and the disorderly abuse of spiritual gifts (14:26-33).

(3) Isaiah spoke of the foreign language of the Assyrian which was "strange lips and alien tongues" to those in Jerusalem (v. 11). He was not referring to ecstatic utterances. There is no reason to suppose that Paul was speaking of anything but foreign languages in I Corinthians 14. The quotation from Isaiah 28 helps to identify "tongues" as foreign languages.

(4) The priests and the prophets erred in their vision and stumbled in giving judgment. Their delusions came from an intoxication with their own cleverness and the stimulation of strong drink. The Corinthian Christians likewise were still babes in understanding, and spiritually ignorant because they were intoxicated by their own importance brought on by a pride of spiritual gifts (14:37-38).

(5) Just as Isaiah described the priest and the prophet gatherings as drunken parties where they were reeling, staggering, confusion and filthiness (vs. 7-8), Paul described the Corinthian assembly as boisterous (14:23), confused (14:40) and devoid of understanding (14:19). Paul said that they were acting in such a way that outsiders would think them mad (14:23).

The phrase, "tongues are for a sign to unbelievers," is the key to understanding the relationship between Isaiah 28 and I Corinthians 14.

In Isaiah, the priests and the prophets did not highly regard the word of the Lord given by Isaiah. In pride they thought their own prophetic cleverness stimulated by strong drink would guide them and improve thei. political fortunes. The foreign tongues of the Assyrians would be a sign to them because of their unbelief in the plain prophecies of Isaiah. The tongue sign was to the people of God who were unbelievers and despised prophesying.

In I Corinthians 14, the "tongue speakers" did not highly regard prophecy from the Lord. They felt the understandable gift of prophecy was a gift inferior to the gift of tongues. In pride they thought their gift used in a highly emotional and confused assembly would guide them into greater spiritual insights. The foreign tongues used so extensively at Corinth in their assembly were in reality a sign of their unbelief of plain prophecy. Like the priests and prophets of Isaiah, the "tongues were for a sign to the people of God who despised prophecy."

The main lesson of I Corinthians 14:1-19 is that prophecy is superior to tongues. The particular lesson of verses 20-25 is that tongue speaking instead of being a sign of spiritual growth is a sign of babyhood. Instead of being a sign of spiritual understanding, it was a sign of spiritual confusion. Instead of being a sign of belief, it was a sign of unbelief.

Would to God that those who delight in such "spiritual exercises" today would hear the word of God in this passage.

The fourth section of chapter fourteen deals with directions for the use of the spiritual gifts in the assembly. There are two principles which apply to the *glossa* gift:

First, the exercise of any spiritual gift in the assembly must be for edifying the whole congregation. *"Let all things be done unto edifying."* Paul said.[72] If it does not edify, it is not

72. I Corinthians 14:26.

to be allowed. The exercise of the *glossa* gift is therefore prohibited unless an interpreter is present. Even with an interpreter only one was allowed to speak at a time. Not more than two or three were allowed at any meeting. By laying down such rules Paul sought to correct the unedifying abuse of tongues at Corinth.

Second, the exercise of any spiritual gift must be done in an orderly fashion. No more than one person was to speak at a time. They were to take turns speaking. The one not speaking was to listen. Paul realized some of the more enthusiastic ones might claim they had no control over the gift and demand to speak any time the Spirit prompted him. Paul corrects this false concept. He said, *"the spirits of the prophets are subject to the prophets."*[73] His final exhortation in the chapter is *"let all things be done decently and in order."*[74]

In chapter fourteen Paul shows that the *glossa* gift is inferior to prophecy and should not be exercised without interpretation. He strikes a death blow to the arrogant possessors of the *glossa* gift by showing that tongues were not a sign of spirituality but of unbelief. By regulating the exercising of the *glossa* gift, he sought to make it edifying and orderly.

In chapters 12-14 Paul deals with these problems that were facing the Corinthian church. He spoke of a time when the *glossa* gift along with the other spiritual gifts would cease. Mature Christians and a mature church do not need such gifts that were given to a special few in a special way at a special time for a special purpose.

73. I Corinthians 14:32.
74. I Corinthians 14:40.

CHAPTER 10

THE PASSING OF SUPERNATURAL GIFTS

The *glossa* gift in the New Testament—along with other miraculous signs—served their purpose and passed away. Their purpose was to confirm the man and his message as being from God. The abuse of the *glossa* gift caused tongues to be a sign of unbelief in the church at Corinth. The perversion of the gift brought a perversion of its purpose. What was intended to be a sign to confirm God's new revelation became a sign of an evil heart of unbelief in Corinth where the gift was abused. The possession of a supernatural gift does not guarantee spirituality. Corinth proves this.

Exercising the *glossa* gift is not a sign of anything today. The gift no longer exists. Since the gift does not exist, neither can its abuse exist. This does not mean that the *glossa* gift is no longer claimed. It is. Men are being deceived into believing that they possess the real gift. This can not be. Such is no longer possible if one accepts the testimony of the Scripture. What is passing for the *glossa* gift today is no more than a psychological phenomenon which finds expression in ecstatic utterances. It is a counterfeit of the real thing. It is a delusion of the devil.

The Need of the Gift Ceased

The purpose of the miraculous gifts was to confirm the revelation of God.[1] Signs accompanied Jesus to confirm his

---

1. Hebrews 2:3-4.

Messiahship.[2] Signs accompanied the preaching of the gospel by apostles and prophets.[3] Unless there is another Jesus or another gospel, signs are not needed.

It is true that men will arise claiming to be Christ. They will try to deceive with signs. They are not to be believed.[4]

It is true that men will teach a perverted gospel, claiming a supernatural message from angels. They are to be anathema.[5]

God's revelation of himself in Jesus Christ is sufficient. There is no need for another Christ to come. No signs are needed to confirm a new Christ. God's revelation of his will in the Scriptures is sufficient. No new scripture needs to be added. No signs are needed to confirm new Scripture.

Means of Obtaining Gifts Ceased

Genuine miraculous gifts, such as "tongue speaking," can not exist today. The means by which they were obtained are no longer available.

On the day of Pentecost and at the household of Cornelius[6] men spoke in tongues after receiving the baptism of the Holy Spirit. These are the only two examples of Holy Spirit baptism in the New Testament. It was received by the apostles on Pentecost when the church was established. It was received by Cornelius and his household when the gospel was first preached to the Gentiles. The baptism of the Holy Spirit was never promised to others. There is no record of it being received

2. John 20:31.
3. Mark 16:19-20.
4. Matthew 24:24.
5. Galatians 1:6-8.
6. Acts 2:1-5; 10:44-46.

by others. The external signs of the baptism of the Holy Spirit
were (1) visible "tongues–like as fire," (2) audible "sound as of
the rushing of a mighty wind," and (3) speaking with "other
tongues as the Spirit gave them utterance." The baptism of
the Holy Spirit was not in order to be saved. Neither was it a
sign of salvation. It was a sign to show the sanction of God upon the activities of men when the gospel was first revealed to
Jews and Gentiles.

The New Testament tells how men were able to speak with
"tongues" and exercise other miraculous gifts after they had
received the laying on of the apostles' hands.

Paul laid his hands on twelve men baptized at Ephesus who
then spoke with tongues.[7] Paul laid hands on Timothy in order that he might receive a gift of God.[8] Philip the evangelist
received the laying on of the apostles' hands[9] and was able to
work signs.[10] He could not transfer this power of working
signs to other people. It was necessary for the apostles to come
down from Jerusalem to do this.[11] This was understood by
those who saw the signs.

*Now when Simon saw that through the laying on of the
apostles' hands the Holy Spirit was given . . . .*[12]

There are no apostles today to bestow these miraculous
gifts. The baptism of Holy Spirit is not in existence today.
Since these are the only two means by which the gift of
tongues was received, the conclusion is evident. There can be
no genuine gift of "tongue speaking" today as it was known in

7. Acts 19:6.
8. II Timothy 1:6.
9. Acts 6:6.
10. Acts 8:6.
11. Acts 8:14-15.
12. Acts 8:18.

the New Testament times. The gift ceased because the means ceased.

Paul Predicted the End of Gifts

He pointed beyond the time of miraculous gifts to a period when tongues would cease and knowledge and prophecy would pass away.

> *Love never faileth: but whether there be prophecies, they shall be done away; whether there be tongues, they shall cease; whether there be knowledge, it shall be done away. For we know in part, and we prophesy in part; but when that which is perfect is come, that which is in part shall be done away.*"[13]

Miraculous gifts were needed when the revelation of God was incomplete. They were to pass when that which is perfect is come.

Three things show that the miraculous gifts of the New Testament—including "tongue speaking"—no longer exist: (1) The need of such gifts ceased. (2) The means of obtaining such gifts ceased. (3) An inspired man predicted that such gifts would cease.

Any one of these points is sufficient to show that the "tongue speaking" phenomenon today is not the same as that in the New Testament. The psychological phenomenon of ecstatic utterances that is called "tongue speaking" today is in reality a counterfeit of the genuine gift that is spoken of in the New Testament. The present phenomenon does not come from the Holy Spirit. It comes either from man's own unconsciousness or an unholy spirit.

13. I Corinthians 13:8-10.

CHAPTER 11

PSYCHOLOGY AND GLOSSOLALIA

A Product of the Times

In times of crisis and rapid change, people panic. Like drowning men, they grab for any straw they see upon the water. The present decade is such a time of crisis. Men have grown desperate in the quest for meaning in life. They need faith to cope with their problems. If faith is missing, man is miserable. When a man does not know what to believe in, he can be led to accept an irrational faith.

A desperate situation exists in the world. The old problems of war, prejudice and oppression still exist. New problems of overpopulation and pollution threaten. It is a time of crisis.

There is little hope left for a person who has absorbed the "God is dead" philosophy of our culture. There can be little moral stability left for a person who believes that the old standards must give way to a "new morality." One can not possess a vital faith who has accepted the statement "it doesn't make much difference what you believe." Three short statements describe the present crisis in our culture. "Matter is the only thing that matters! Now is the only time that counts! Self is the only valid concern!"

At such a time as this men grab for straws. Contemporary

man is a vacuum seeking to be made full. Numerous delusions surround him. The vacuum made in man for God is too often filled with the devil's substitutes. Astrology is such a substitute. There is a renewal of this ancient substitution which men have long used to excape responsibility. Drugs are another devil substitute. They offer false hope. Drugs do not change reality. They only make man into a thing--uncaring and unwilling. Perverted sex, sadistic violence and Spiritualism may be added to this list of delusions which the devil used to lure desperate men into false hope.

One of the most deceptive delusions of the devil is "experiential religion." It has become a popular substitution for the real religion of Jesus Christ as revealed in the Scriptures. Faith has been substituted by feeling. The Christ of history has been substituted by the Jesus of experience. The all sufficient Scriptures have been substituted by supernatural directions and miraculous divine intervention.

Glossolalia is a prominent part of "experiential religion" among some groups. The tensions of our time make it attractive. The weakness of the Christian witness makes such a substitute even more alluring. These two factors, coupled with the vacuum in a life devoid of spirituality, create an ideal climate for the intrusion of glossolalia. It is the author's judgment that these three factors are the basic reasons for the resurgence of glossolalia in this decade.

Dodds comments on phenomena similar to glossolalia which had a prominent place in the Greek world during the Archaic age.

In a guilt-culture, the need for supernatural assurance, for an authority transcending man's, appears to be overwhelmingly strong . . . . Without Delphi, Greek society could scarcely have endured the tensions to which it was subjected in the Archaic Age . . . . The Greeks believed in their Oracle, not because they were superstitious fools,

> *but because they could not do without believing in it*
> *.... (speaking of Dionysus ecstasy) The aim of his cult*
> *was ecstasis—which again could mean anything from*
> *"taking you out of yourself" to a profound alteration of*
> *personality. And its psychological function was to satis-*
> *fy and relieve the impulse to reject responsibility, an im-*
> *pulse which exists in all of us and can become under cer-*
> *tain social conditions an irresistible craving.*[1]

A culture full of tensions seeks divine assurance in experiential ways. If such does not come through the means provided by God for man in the Scriptures, it will come through means of man's own devising.

Pattison makes this same observation in his excellent study of the glossolalia phenomenon. He explains the resurgence of glossolalia in the seventeenth and eighteenth centuries as a reaction against rationalistic religion:

> *Dissatisfied with the intellectual rational concepts of*
> *religion, the pietists looked for direct human evidence*
> *for the existence and activity of God. Thus seizures,*
> *trances, automatistic behavior, and glossolalia were*
> *now taken to be manifestations of possession of God.*[2]

Pattison also shows how the occurrence of glossolalia in traditional Christian groups in the eighteenth and nineteenth centuries came when "experiential component of religious experience had been replaced by a chiefly intellectual religious practice."[3] Glossolalia was the means of establishing an experiential base for religious faith.

1. E. R. Dodds, The Greeks and the Irrational (Boston: Beacon Press, 1957), pp. 75, 77.
2. E. Mansell Pattison, "Behavioral Science Research on the Nature of Glossolalia," Journal of the American Scientific Affiliation, Vol. 20, No. 3 (September, 1968), p. 74.
3. Ibid.

Instead of glossolalia being interpreted as a sign from heaven, it could more appropriately be interpreted as a sign of the times. Glossolalia resurges in popularity during times of religious persecution, times of great social and cultural stresses, and times of cold, rationalistic, religious formalism.

Psychological Causes of Glossolalia

Through the study of the history of glossolalia and observations from case histories, this author has observed a pattern. Three things seem to be in the background of individuals who experience glossolalia outside socio-cultural groups like the Pentecostals. In such groups it is the normal expectation in conversion.

First, the individual had suppressed religious feelings. He had been hesitant to speak of his faith. Oates sees the glossolalia experience stemming from a silence about religion in everyday conversation. He writes:

" *The easy spontaneous discussion of religions particularly in its intimate personal aspects no longer exists. . . . The milieu in which we live has become overwhelmingly inarticular about God.*"[4]

Not only does this lack of communicating faith exist in individual experiences, it is to be found also in the religious group. With churches caught up in social, political and materialistic affairs, discussion of spiritual themes are pushed to the background. Oates observes:

Churches have contributed to the silence about personal faith . . . . It has become more of a social gathering and the social dialogue between members has tended to be about social and civic affairs rather than upon religious experiences . . . . The formulation and discussion of

4. Frank Stagg, E. Glenn Henson and Wayne E. Oates, Glossolalia: Tongue Speaking in Biblical, Historical and Psychological Perspective (Nashville: Abington Press, 1967), p. 79.

religious questions is not the substances of the "after meeting" conversations and communications.[5]

Contemporary social situations and even church associations are such that religious topics are avoided. Deep religious feelings are suppressed and find no release in expression. Confession of sin is taboo. Religious questions are left unasked and relevant spiritual themes are too often not discussed. In our present time desperate human beings are crying out from their depth to be heard in depth. But it seems that no one is listening and no one cares. Expression of such deep personal religious feelings seems to be passe.

Second, the individual had deep unresolved spiritual tension. These tensions often are in the form of moral inconsistency, family and financial difficulties, faith problems and materialism.

Bergsma sees the glossolalia experience rising from such tensions and inner conflicts in an individual. He says:

The drawing power of the glossolalia movement among the present day intellectual types is the unconscious need all people have to solve their personality conflicts, to shed their feelings of inadequacy and guilt.[6]

Pattison shows that glossolalia is to be normal in situations when the experience is practiced as a part of the expected ritual. He suggests, however, that:

in situations where glossolalia is not a cultural expectation, or the group is already part of a deviant subculture, we would expect to find a correlation between glossolalia and psychopathology.[7]

5. Ibid., p. 80.
6. Stuart Bergsma, Speaking with Tongues, (Grand Rapids; Baker Book House, 1965), p. 16.
7. Pattison op. cit., p. 76.

Glossolalia has long been studied as a psychological phenomenon brought on through severe stress, hypnotism, autohypnotism and mental illness. Other causes can be given for the phenomenon, but unresolved spiritual tension must be considered a major contributing factor in a majority of the cases.

When a person's life style runs contrary to his ideals, severe personality conflicts are produced. Tensions build up in the subconscious to a great degree of intensity. Sometimes these tensions are released through drugs, sex and violence. The cathartic experience of highly emotional religious excitement such as glossolalia may be used to release the tensions. In both situations tensions are released, but the solution is inadequate and temporary.

The problem is a spiritual one and must be resolved through spiritual means dictated in the Scriptures. There must be repentance—genuine and from the heart. There must be confession—open and without excuse. Forgiveness must be sought of God through the means he has set in the Scriptures—whether baptism or prayer. Finally the grace of God in forgiveness must be accepted and a new life begun. One can not solve spiritual tensions through physical means. One must not seek cheap grace through psychologically induced religious ecstasy.

It is easier to get caught up in religious excitement than to repent. It is less humbling to seek and find a new way of divine grace and call the old way inadequate, than it is to admit error before the people one has wronged. No doubt one of the reasons for the popularity of glossolalia is that it promises a way to "instant salvation," "cheap grace," and "immediate spirituality." Spiritual tensions are resolved temporarily without having to do it God's way. The ego is not hurt so much this way. Hear this parable.

A Parable

John Christian takes a wrong road in the journey of life. He travels the road for a while. All of the time other Christians are telling him that he is going the wrong way. Finally, he sees that he is lost. He wants to get back on the right road, but he does not want to face those whose counsel he has rejected. He does not want to go back to the place where he made the wrong turn and start all over again. He knows some would jeer and say, "I told you so." What is he to do?

He sees another turn in the road. There is a sign at the turn that says that the road leads back to the road he originally left. It is supposed to be a short cut. John Christian takes the road with joy. He believes he can get back to the right road without backtracking and eating humble pie. He is enthusiastic about the road. His ego is preserved. He has found a short cut and is anxious to tell others about it. Little does he know that it leads farther and farther away from God. He feels right about the road and with the help of new found friends is able to interpret the road maps to fit the way he wants to go.

When other Christians try to show him that he is again taking the wrong road, he criticizes their narrowness. He feels that he is their spiritual superior. He finally quits talking with other Christians. He has found new friends. He marches to a different drum beat. He sings a different song.

John accomplished two things. He resolved his tensions. He preserved his ego. But does he realize where the road leads?

Third, the individual had an impoverished spiritual life. This does not mean that he forsook worship services, he just neglected to worship. This does not mean that he refused to read his Bible, he just did not apply it to his personal life. This does not mean he never said his prayers, he just did not know God in personal devotion.

Is the church to blame for this? Is a man impoverished spiritually because of the dullness of the worship, the deadness of
the church and the coldness of the spiritual fellowship? Not
necessarily. Man is responsible for his own spiritual growth.
He can not blame others for his weakness. Often the church is
made the scape goat for one's own personal neglect. If he
fails to feel a nearness to God in his worship, perhaps it is his
own empty heart rather than the coldness of the ritual. If he
does not know the joy of salvation, perhaps it is his own lack
of faith rather than the church's lack of spirituality. When one
finds he is unspiritual, it is easier to lay the blame on others
than to repent.

The church must not be excused for its weakness in leading
its members to a more spiritual life. Christians assemble to be
edified. If they are not edified, there must be something wrong.
A statement found in M'Clintock-Strong Cyclopedia published
in 1891 illustrates this point. Under the article entitled, "Gift
of Tongues" is this comment:

> *This might be the only way in which some natures could
> be aroused out of sensual life or the dullness of formal
> ritual. The ecstasy of adoration which seemed to men
> madness might be refreshment unspeakable to one who
> was weary with the subtle questionings of the intellect,
> to whom all familiar and intelligible words were fraught
> with recollections of controversial bitterness of the wan-
> derings of doubt.*[8]

Pattison points out that the glossolalia phenomenon arises
in times of rationalism in religious teaching and formalism in
religious ritual. His evaluation of the contemporary glossolalia movement is this:

8. John M Clintock and James Strong, Cyclopaedia of Biblical,
theological and Ecclesiastical Literature, Vol. 10 (New York: Harper
and Brothers, publishers, 1892), p.483.

In the staid main-line churches of America, the function of glossolalia seems to fit more into a means of protest. It can also be seen as a recurrent infusion of experiential religion into denominations that have become mainly intellectual enterprises. [9]

Whether the blame rests upon the individual or the church is not for this author to determine. The point is that an impoverished spiritual life is to be found in the background of those who have experienced glossolalia when it is not a cultural expectation.

Pattison shows three ways in which glossolalia can be induced in an individual. (1) It can be a by-product of psychotic disorganization. (2) It can be a mechanism of expression in neurotic conflicts. (3) It can be an exercise brought about because it is the normal expected thing in certain socio-cultural circumstances. Pattison further suggests:

. . . the phenomenon of glossolalia per se can not be interpreted necessarily as either deviant or pathological, for its meaning is determined and must be interpreted in terms of the socio-cultural context. [10]

Ample evidence indicates that glossolalia can result from different stimuli. It is explainable in terms of man's own psyche. To attribute it to a divine gift is to ignore evidence to the contrary. Pattison comments:

. . . there is a wealth of reasonable data which gives us an outline of the psychological, social, and cultural contexts within which glossolalia can be and is produced. Thus we need not invoke either divine or devilish supernatural forces to explain or justify the existence and

9. Pattison, op. cit., p. 75.
10. Ibid., p. 76.

function of glossolalia.[11]

Significance of Glossolalia to the Group

The glossolalia phenomenon is the same throughout the world. Whether it is practiced by Spiritualists, Moslems, Episcopalians or Pentecostals, the experience is the same in origin, physical characteristics and psychological value. The significance of glossolalia to the group differs according to the culture and circumstance. Pattison shows four different ways in which glossolalia is regarded.

First, glossolalia is regarded by some to be a reaction to rationalism in religion. When worship has degenerated into cold ritual and faith has degenerated into proved propositions, religion loses its meaning to man. There is no vitality or feeling connected with religious exercise. God is depersonalized. Service becomes duty. When religion reaches such a state the experiential base to religion must be re-established. This is true in the Islam religion.[12] This has been true in the history of Christianity. A common expression of experiential religions is glossolalia.

Second, glossolalia is regarded in some places as a sign of religious leadership and correctness of doctrine. Pattison says:

> *In the corgo cults of Melanesia, the glossolalia likewise verifies the charismatic leader's claim to authority. This seems to be a major social function of glossolalia as practiced by many shamans and priests as reported in many ethnographies.*[13]

If the gods possess a man to take over his speech, then it

11. Ibid., p. 84.
12. See page 75f.
13. Pattison, op. cit., p. 75.

indicates that the man is the messenger of God and speaks the truth. This function of glossolalia is demonstrated in the Greek culture by the fact that the oracles of Apollo at Delphi were highly regarded.

Third, glossolalia as it is practiced among the neo-Pentecostals seems to serve as a means of protest against the main-line churches of America. The neo-Pentecostal literature indicates dissatisfaction with materialism in the churches, the organizational structures of the denominations, the lack of vitality in witnessing and the dullness of the religious ceremonies. Glossolalia is a protest against all of these things.

Fourth, glossolalia among present day Pentecostals seems to stem from their socio-economic position in society. Pattison suggests that their "ecstatic behavior is both an outlet for repressed conflicts, and a means of justifying one's unique position in society as a possessor of truth and righteousness."[14]

An added function of glossolalia is all of the groups mentioned above is recruitment. It serves as a method of winning new members and identifying them into a common unit through the glossolalia experience. The glossolalia experience is that which separates the "in-sider" from the "out-sider." It is the common experience which binds men of radically different backgrounds and conflicting doctrinal teachings into a special brotherhood.

It has been this author's observation that the fellowship tie that exists between glossolalists is much stronger than their religious ties within the church of which they are a part. This is true even when their fellow glossolalists believe a radically different doctrine and practices conflicitng religious ceremonies.

14. Ibid.

It should be noted that there is no evidence that the glosso-lalia experience produces spirituality. James writes:

> *They undoubtedly have no essential spiritual significance, and although their presence makes his conversion more memorable to the convert, it has never been proved that converts who show them are more presevering or fertile in good fruits than those whose change of heart has had less violent accompaniments. On the whole, uncon-sciousness, convulsions, visions, involuntary vocal utter-ances, and suffocation, must be simply ascribed to the subject's having a large subliminal region, involving ner-vous instability.* [15]

Advocates of glossolalia contend that the experience does bring about change in the individual's spiritual life. The ex-perience has an emotional value by bringing a sense of joy. It is claimed that the experience produces a transformed life and enables one to cope with the totality of existence.[16] It can not be shown, however, that these same fruits are not produced by those whose conversion and commitment is not accompanied by such irrational exercise. Pattison says:

> *Glossolalia does not miraculously change people in a supernatural sense, but participating in glossolalia as a part of a larger social and personal commitment may play an important role in the change of direction in partici-pants' lives.* [17]

It is not the experience, but the context in which the exper-ience occurs that produces moral and ethical changes.

15. William James, The Varities of Religious Experience (New York: The New American Library, 1958), p. 201.

16. Morton T. Kelsey, Tongue Speaking (Garden City: Doubleday and Company, 1964), p. 3.

17. Pattison, op. cit., p. 85.

The Speech of Glossolalia

Kelsey gives a good description of glossolalia speech as it is practiced among neo-Pentecostals.

> *The speech itself rises in an effortless flow of unusually complex structure, with the repetition and inflection characteristic of language. It is neither controlled nor directly understood by the speaker, but takes possession of his speech. While occasionally a listener can identify a foreign language known to him, but not to the speaker the meaning is almost always spoken by an interpretation.*[18]

Glossolalia speech must be considered as one of several different types of motor automatism. Myers says:

> *I begin, then, with my definition of automatism, as the widest term under which to include the range of subliminal emergences into ordinary life. Different classes of those uprushes have arleady received special names. The turbulent uprush and downdraught of hysteria; the helpful uprushes of genius, the profound and recuperative changes which follow on hypnotic suggestion . . . . But the main mass of subliminal manifestations remain undescribed. I have dealt little with veridical hallucinations, not at all with automatic writing nor with the utterances of spontaneous trance. The products of inner audition I term sensory automatisms. The messages conveyed by movement of limbs or hand or tongue, initiated by an inner motor impulse beyond the conscious will— these are what I term motor automatisms.*[19]

Myers shows from case histories that both glossolalia and automatic writing are but different forms of the same thing—

18. Kelsey, op. cit., p. 1.
19. F. W. Myers, Human Personality and its Survival of Bodily Death (New Hyde Park, New York: University Books, Inc., 1961), pp. 162-63.

the subliminal emergences which produce visible or audible activities which are not under the control of the conscious ego. Both automatic writing and glossolalia are used by spirit mediums. Sometimes the automatic speech is understood and sometimes it is not understood.[20] The same can be said of automatic writing.[21]   Little is said about the religious aspect of motor automations in Myers'study. He is primarily concerned with spirit mediums, abnormal psychology and other types of phenomena which show evidence of mysterious activities going on in the subconscious part of man. It is interesting to note that the same kinds of things that are to be found in glossolalia and its accompanying activities also are found completely outside of religious influence. The phenomena is the same, but the interpretation placed upon them is vastly different. The glossolalist claims his speech is from God. The Spiritualist claims the phenomenon is from spirits of the dead. The psychologist claims that it comes from man's own subconscious.

A curious case of automatic writing is to be found in the "Oahspe Bible." Dr. John B. Newbrough first published this "Bible" in 1882. In the preface the following account is given:

> *The years between 1871 and 1881 were spent in spiritual purification during which time he became aware of spiritguidance. Instructed to purchase a typewriter, which had been just invented, he did so. Upon sitting on the instrument an hour before dawn he discovered that his hands typed without his conscious control. In fact he was not aware of what his hands typed unless he read what was being printed. He was told that he was to write a book—but must not read what he was writing until it was completed. At the end of the year when the manuscript was completed he was instructed to read and publish the book titled Oahspe, a New Bible.*[22]

20. Ibid., pp. 293ff.
21. Ibid., p. 323.
22. John Ballaw Newbrough, Oahspe a New Bible (Los Angeles: Kosmon Press, 1929), p. iv.

Automatic writing and automatic speech in glossolalia are to be explained the same way. They are products of man's own sub-conscience. The interpretation of automatic speech and writing differs according to the circumstances in which it is found. If one claims that such comes from God, how can the same phenomenon be explained in spirit mediums, writers of new bibles and abnormal psychology?

A number of recent studies have been made on the speech of glossolalia. Pattison brings a number of these together in his excellent article in the Journal of American Scientific Affiliation.[23] From these studies four things can be shown: (1) The speech is not foreign language. (2) The speech is learned and perfected by practice. (3) It can be imitated in the laboratory without being detected by those accustomed to hearing glossolalia. (4) The speech has certain characteristics of children's speech.

The speech is not a foreign language. Sounds similar to foreign phrases are sometimes uttered either by accident or from the memory storehouse of the subconscious mind. Walker writes about the latter alternative:

> *When the mind is under the influence of some powerful external force, when the unconscious self is roused to activity, when the powers of memory are subjected to an abnormal stimulus, foreign languages, the words of which have fallen on the ears of the subject without any conscious attention on his part, and have again without any consciousness of it on his part been impressed on his memory, may be clearly uttered.*[24]

The same phenomenon can be observed in subjects under

23. Pattison, op. cit., p. 76-78.
24. Dawson Walker, The Gift of Tongues (Edinburgh: T & T Clark, 1906), p. 59.

hypnosis or under anesthetic. The subconscious mind is such that it can recall events and words which the conscious mind has totally forgotten.

The glossolalia speech is learned by practice. Pattison says:

> *Several linguistic studies, including our own, suggest that glossolalists develop their glossolalic speech from ill-formed structure to "practiced" and "polished" glossolalic speech. Thus the linguistic qualities of the glossolalia depends to some extent on the stage of development of glossolalia.*[25]

Many glossolalists like to practice their vocabulary and add new sounds to their speech.

One does not have to be a glossolalist to produce glossolalic speech. Al Carlson at the University of California recorded the speech of glossolalists during their spiritual exercise. Later he recorded the speech of non-glossolalist volunteers whom he asked to speak spontaneously in an unknown language. Glossolalists were asked to rate the different recordings. They were unable to distinguish them. A similar test was made by Werner Cohn of the University of British Columbia with identical results.[26]

It has long been observed that glossolalia is similar to the speech of children in many ways. Some have suggested that glossolalia is a "regression to an early mode of speech in which vocalization is used for purposes other than just the communication of rational thought."[27] It appears that children utter their gibberish for the sheer joy of uttering sound. Could this be true of the glossolalist?

25. Pattison, op. cit., p. 77.
26. Ibid., p. 78.
27. Ibid., p. 77.

In modern glossolalia speech the interpretation serves an important function. The interpreter must not be confused with a translator. He is not translating a language; he is rather trying to give meaning to meaningless sounds uttered by the glossolalist. Of course the whole thing is very subjective. Sometimes a whole paragraph in English is translated from a brief utterance of glossolalic speech. Sometimes a glossolalic utterance will be translated in different ways at different times. The role of the interpreter then is not translation but giving the meaning of untranslatable sounds. Usually the interpretation is that which confirms the sanction of God on the action of the group.

Pattison summarized his linguistic studies of glossolalia by saying:

> *Glossolalia has specific linguistic structure based on the language tongue of the speaker, that the linguistic organization is limited, and that the capacity to speak in this type of semi-organized language can be replicated under experimental conditions. Thus glossolalia does not appear to be a "strange language," but rather the aborted formation of familiar language.*[28]

Case Histories

In his own counselling experience, the author has worked with individuals who have experienced glossolalia and similar psychological experiences. There is nothing wrong with the experience itself. It is a psychological phenomenon prompted by various stimuli to certain types of persons. At times, like the use of drugs, hypnosis and shock treatment, it may be helpful psychologically. The error comes when one identifies this experience as being directly from God rather than from his own psyche.

28. Pattison, op. cit., p. 78.

Case No. 1: Mary B. seemed to seek such an experience to escape the responsibility of making her own decisions. If she were led by the spirit to do something, she would not be to blame if she failed. The psychological experience released some of her nervous tensions, but it also left an undesirable side effect. She began to withdraw from making rational decisions and began to depend upon her psychological experiences to guide her.

God never asked anyone to give up his will in order to have a psychological experience. Man's will must always be in control. Paul recognized this when he wrote to the Corinthians who possessed different miraculous spiritual gifts. He said: *"The spirits of the prophets are subject to the prophets."* [29]

When one wills to submit to Jesus, it is not an abandonment of his own will. It is rather an exercising of his will. When he surrenders to Jesus he knows who his master is and specifically what he surrenders to, since it is revealed objectively in the Scriptures. When one surrenders his will to a mystical, unknown force, it is dangerous. One cannot know if the spirit that takes control of the will is a Holy Spirit or an unholy spirit. Subjective personal feelings can not tell whether the experience is a divine reality or a counterfeit of the devil. Paul warns Christians that *"such men are false prophets, deceitful workers, fashioning themselves into apostles of Christ and no marvel, for even Satan fashioneth himself into an angel of light."* [30]

Objectivity is impossible when the will is surrendered. Subjective personal experience can not determine truth from error. Bishop James Pike sincerely believed that he talked to his dead son. His evidence for this belief was a subjective experience. Such can not stand the objective test of the Scriptures

29. I Corinthians 14:32.
30. II Corinthians 11:13-14.

The rich man in Jesus' parable wanted Lazarus to go back from the grave and warn his five brethren lest they end up as he did. The statement of Abraham was: *"They have Moses and the prophets. Let them hear them . . . . If they hear not Moses and the prophets, neither will they be persuaded if one rise from the dead."*[31]

The Christian must always be on guard against the deceit-fulness of the devil. There will always be false teachers claiming to work wonders. There will always be those who believe them. Paul was dealing with such a problem when he warned the Christians at Thessalonica:

> *Whose coming is according to the working of Satan, with all power and signs and lying wonders, and with all deceit of righteousness for them that perish, because they receive not the love of the truth that they might be saved. And for this cause God sendeth them a working of error that they should believe a lie, that they all might be judged who believe not the truth but have pleasure in unrighteousness.*[32]

The devil uses subjective experiences to get a man to abandon his will. He promises a greater faith. He claims that he can give one spiritual maturity. The promise is a lie. The claim is false. The Scriptures say faith comes by hearing the word of God rather than experiences.[33] The Scriptures also say that Christian growth comes from receiving the milk of the word rather than from subjective emotional experiences.[34]

Man is responsible. He must not abandon his will. He

31. Luke 16:29, 31.
32. II Thessalonians 2:9-12.
33. Romans 10:17.
34. II Peter 2:2.

chooses whom he will serve. He decides which road he will take.[35] He works out his own salvation.[36] It is the folly of Esau to sell the birthright of reason for the pottage of a psychological experience.

Case No. 2: Anita H. seemed to seek such an experience in reaction to a legalistic, materialistic and impoverished spiritual life that she had formerly led. She was to be pitied. Her spiritual life had been so void she needed to conjure up an emotional experience in order to have a sense of the Divine presence.

The materialism of our time and the lack of personal spiritual depth is a major contributing factor to the growth of the glossolalia phenomenon. The surest way to refute the false doctrine and stop the practice of glossolalia is to develop greater devotion and spirituality in the life and the work of the church.

The alternative of materialism and spiritual shallowness in the life and the work of the church is not glossolalia. Such a cure would be worse than the disease it strives to overcome. A dead secular church is wrong. So also is a live pseudo-spiritual church based on error. One cannot correct error by substituting another error.

The Pharisees of Jesus' day would: *"Compass sea and land to make one proselyte, and when he is become so, ye make him twofold more a son of hell than yourselves.*[37] In a similar way advocates of glossolalia seek to proselyte people from legalism and materialism only to make their spiritual condition worse.

35. Matthew 7:13.
36. Philippines 2:12.
37. Matthew 23:15.

Examining one's own life in the light of the word of God
and finding that he has become legalistic, materialistic and
spiritually impoverished can be the first step in spiritual growth.
It is not a comfortable feeling. It brings on despair. At this
point God wants a person to repent—to change his life. The
weaknesses of the past must be faced and overcome. This is
difficult to do. It is hard on the ego. It requires all of the
strength one's will can muster. One has to learn that he can
not depend upon himself. He needs to seek and find the help
that God gives in Jesus Christ.

It would be much easier to try to escape the problem than
face it. Sometimes this is done by "instant religion" of which
glossolalia is a part. Instead of the hard work of repentance,
one takes the easy road of an emotional experience. It inflates the ego to think that God has given him a special gift.

Case No. 3: Bill J. sought the glossolalia experience as a
short cut to spiritual maturity. He seemed to want "cheap
grace" and "instant spiritual maturity." He was frustrated because the ideals he was seeking seemed beyond his reach. The
glossolalia experience gave a delusion of intimacy with God
along with a spiritual superiority. He sought and obtained it.

There are no short cuts to spirituality. There is no "cheap
grace". The gate is always straight and the way is always nar-
row.[38] Religion is not a one-time experience, but a day-by-
day living. Certainly it is frustrating to live below the ideals
that one is seeking. This is where Christian growth comes in.
A child does not reach manhood in a day. Neither does a
Christian reach maturity in a one-time experience. It requires
diligence. Christian graces must be added. Perfecting trials
must be endured. Christian food must be consumed. All of

38. Matthew 7:13-14.

this is in the maturing process and takes time. There are no short cuts.

Luke tells of a Christian who tried to purchase spiritual gifts by money. Simon had one time been a sorcerer but had become a Christian. He wanted to purchase the gift that belonged only to the apostles. The rebuke of Peter is plain. He said that "Simon was *"in the gall of bitterness and the bond of iniquity."*[39] His heart was not right in the sight of God. He needed to pray for forgiveness.

Those who seek the gifts that belong only to the apostolic age have the same problem as Simon. Their heart is not right in the sight of God, and they need to pray for forgiveness.

Case No. 4: Bill S. was a very confused young man. Because of glossolalia and other experiences that he thought were from God, he attempted to seduce a Christian young lady to immorality. He justified his own lasciviousness because he felt that God had given him the go ahead.

When the will breaks down through rational abandonment and emotional stimulation, normal ethical barriers are easily overcome. How many crimes have been done in the name of religion by men who have confused a devil delusion for a divine illusion! How many times in history has religion been used as a tool to manipulate people! Unscrupulous men will not hesitate to stir up the religious inclinations in order to pervert them for their own gain.

One cannot afford to let emotions rule over reason. Personal subjective feeling must always be tempered by the faith that comes by hearing the Word of God. One of the things

---

39. Acts 8:23.

that makes a man different from the animals is that he has a will. He is in control.

It is not this author's purpose to discuss the subject of demonology. It is sufficient to say, however, that there is as much evidence to indicate that glossolalia is demon possession as there is that it is a Divine possession.

Case No. 5: Jack P. seemed to seek the tongue-speaking experience because of his admiration for one whom he believed to be spiritual. Following his leader he sought to be liberated, only to be brought into captivity of error.

Jack was a recent convert. He was overjoyed when he became a Christian. Someone he admired suggested that obtaining the glossolalia experience would add to his joy and spirituality. He sought the experience and found it. He interpreted the experience as Divine intervention rather than a psychological experience. He believed his leader without checking to see if the doctrine were scriptural.

John warns Christians: *"Believe not every spirit, but prove the spirits whether they are of God, because many false prophets are gone out into the world."*[40]

One never reads of Jesus giving ecstatic utterances or surrendering his will to an emotional experience. Is one to suggest that he was less spiritual because of this? Remember Jesus—not self-appointed prophets—is to be the Christian guide.

The devil twisted Scriptures when he was tempting Jesus in Matthew 4. He suggested that Jesus cast himself from the pinnacle of the temple because God had promised to keep him

40. I John 4:1.

from harm in Psalms 91:11ff: He said, *"He shall give his angels charge concerning thee, and on their hands they shall bear thee up lest haply thou dash thy foot against a stone."*[41] Jesus answered the devil plainly: *"Thou shalt not make trial of the Lord thy God."* Jesus knew that it was wrong for a man to put God to the test in order to satisfy his own whims. This is the lesson that needs to be learned by glossolalists today. A man of faith does not need signs today to confirm his faith. His faith is based upon the testimony of the word of God. He does not make trial of God by asking for a sign.

A statement by C. G. Jung, as quoted by Bernard Martin, serves to explain the psychological phenomenon of tongue speaking: "Spirit communications are generally nothing else than very commonplace manifestations of the personal unconscious."[42] A psychological study of tongue speaking indicates that it is a psychological experience from man's own personal unconsciousness. It is not from heaven but from men.

Conclusion

Psychological observations about glossolalia show it to be an experience that can be produced under controlled circumstances and in predictable ways. It is to be compared to automatic writing and is to be found completely outside of the religious context. The phenomenon is speech resembling that of a child. It can be learned, practiced and polished. Interpretation is not translation, but subjectively giving the meaning of non-translatable sounds. The source of glossolalia is from man's own psyche. The phenomenon is to be found in persons with psychotic and neurotic problems, but it is also found in well-adjusted persons.

41. Matthew 4:6.
42. Bernard Martin, op. cit., p. 99.

There is nothing either good or bad about the experience itself. It is the normal function of certain kinds of minds under certain kinds of circumstances. The error comes when one attributes glossolalia to a miraculous gift of God through the Holy Spirit. The error is attributing something to God which is from man.

The experience can produce a good psychological effect upon a person in the same way that drugs, hypnosis and shock treatments do. Glossolalia can be an integrating emotional experience which helps one cope with the totality of life and its problems. It can increase self-confidence, inspire persons to save, work, cooperate and take risks. It can be a purgative of destructive thought patterns such as jealousy, fear, and hate. Glossolalia does not of itself produce these effects. Under certain circumstances the experience can be psychologically helpful to a person.

The experience can also produce bad effects on an individual. It can produce negative personality traits such as pride, selfishness and egotism. It can be used as an escape from responsibility. It often has become a delusion to the mind of an individual and interpreted as being a miraculous gift of God. By a false religious interpretation it has encouraged men to seek "instant salvation", "cheap grace " and "immedite spirituality." It is often used by the devil as a counterfeit of the real spiritual blessings and experiences that one can know as a Christian.

Glossolalia is a relatively common psychological experience. It is explained in various ways depending upon the religious, cultural and educational background of the subject. The phenomenon is often found in times of stress and change. It may be a helpful purgative experience bringing about a better orientation to life or it may be a destructive escape mechanism to avoid responsibility.

CHAPTER 12

LOGICAL CONSIDERATIONS

The contemporary glossolalia practice must not be regarded as an innocent expression of devotion by individuals seeking a higher spiritual life. It is based on a fundamental doctrinal error and can not be treated lightly. The practice has serious theological consequence in the church and serious spiritual consequences for the individual who practices it.

This is not to say that the practice is wrong of itself. As has already been suggested, it may possess some therapeutic value in certain cases. It is a psychological phenomenon of man and must not be regarded as a Divine gift. The error comes when the experience is attributed to God.

This is not to judge the sincerity of the person who experiences glossolalia. To him, it is a traumatic experience which he interprets as having spiritual significance. This interpretation of the experience may even play an important role in radically changing the life style of the individual. The question is whether the interpretation is true. Experiences that individuals have had in worshiping idols have also brought a change in life style.

The Question of Authority

The question of authority is at the very heart of all religious discussions. Not only must one ask the question:

"By what Scriptural authority is glossolalia practiced?" as in chapters 7-10, one must also ask: "What does the practice of glossolalia do to Scriptural authority?"

Accepting the practice of glossolalia as a miraculous gift from God leads to a denial of the sufficiency of the Scriptures. If glossolalia be from God, then it is new revelation--something God is revealing now which is different from the Scriptures. Whether what is said is revelation in one's native tongue called prophecy or whether it is revelation in another tongue called glossolalia, the results are the same in one respect. God is revealing something different from the Scriptures. Some suggest that glossolalia is not new revelation, but only confirmation of the revelation in the Scriptures.[1] This is to deny clear facts. Advocates of glossolalia claim it is from God. It is evident that it is different from Scripture both in the glossolalia speech and its interpretation. These facts make it logically impossible to deny that it is new revelation.

New revelation from God makes old revelations of God inadequate and incomplete. After the giving of the New Testament through Jesus Christ, the Old Testament Scriptures were no longer adequate and complete as God's revelation to man. It is on this point that Christians differ with Jews. In like manner the giving of new revelation through the glossolalia experience makes the Old and New Testaments inadequate and incomplete as God's revelation to man. It is on this point that glossolalists differ from Christians who accept the Scriptures as their total and sufficient guide.

If the "revelation of God" through the glossolalia experience is new, then it is an addition to God's word revealed in

1. This seems to be the position taken by James Ash in an unpublished paper entitled "A Critique of Restorationist Pneumatology" (January, 1971), p. 1.

the Scriptures. If the "revelation of God" through the glosso-lalia experience is not new revelation--nothing more than Scripture--it is useless.

More and more men are seeing the folly of creeds in religion. They, as man's rational attempt to supplement Scripture, are failures. Creeds divide. Creeds are of man and uninspired. It is folly to tack them on to God's revelation in Scripture as another religious authority. If one can see the folly of a creed, he can see the folly of glossolalia. Glossolalia is man's irrational attempt to supplement Scripture. It, like creeds, divides. It, like creeds, is of man and uninspired. It, like creeds, is a supplement to God's revelation in Scripture and must not be regarded as religious authority.

J. W. Roberts clearly argues for the sufficiency of the Scriptures as opposed to experiences like tongue speaking:

The finality of the Scriptures derives from the "once-for-all-time" nature of the work of Jesus as the Son of God. The incarnation of Jesus -- His becoming flesh -- is not to be repeated. Hebrews 9.26 declares that "once at the end of the ages hath he appeared to put away sin by the sacrifice of himself." His work needs not to be repeated, because it was "once for all."

The word (Greek hapax) for this final, not-to-be-repeated sacrificial work of Jesus is the same word used to describe the revelation of the Word of God. Jude thus spoke of "the faith once for all time delivered to the saints." There is no more need for the continuation of inspiration and revelation after the work was once complete than for a continuation of the dying of Jesus on the cross.[2]

Roberts further adds in summarizing his arguments:

That word (Scriptures) is the church's sole authority

2. J.W. Roberts, "The Finality and Sufficiency of the Holy Scriptures," The Star 1:71 (January, 1971), p. 14.

for all time. Those tempted to substitute their feelings, experiences, or modern revelations should remember that Jesus said, "He that rejecteth me and receiveth not my word hath one which will judge him in the last day. the word that I have spoken will judge him in that day.[3]

Accepting the practice of glossolalia as a miraculous gift from God makes every man's own subjective experience his religious authority. There can be no religious standard for all men if God gives different messages to different men through glossolalia. This is graphically illustrated at the present time by the fact that the practice of glossolalia exists in denominations holding contrary beliefs. If glossolalia and the interpretation of it be from God, why does it not correct the errors of doctrine and practice found in the groups who espouse it?

If different messages are given to different men through glossolalia and its interpretation, there can be no objective religious standard by which everyone is tested. This particularly becomes a knotty problem when an equally sincere Jew, Roman Catholic, Protestant, Mormon and Moslem all experience glossolalia. By what standard is one to determine the real from the counterfeit? All of these different men in one way or another recognize the God of the Bible and believe that they serve him. Accepting the validity of subjective personal religious authority will finally result in putting the objective religious authority of the Scripture in a secondary position.

It is but a short step from the acceptance of the glossolalia experience to the acceptance of latter-day revelation. This is illustrated in Mormonism. The Mormons have practiced speaking in tongues from their beginning. It was from among

3. Ibid.

those who practiced tongue speaking and claimed to possess the other miraculous gifts that Mormonism gained its greatest following on the Western Reserve of the United States. If God uses a man's vocal cords to speak in a tongue, it logically follows that the same vocal cords could be used to utter latter-day revelation. The Book of Mormon is accepted as being from God by the same arguments that are used to show that glossolalia is from God. R. L. Roberts writes:

> *In the Campbell movement those individuals and churches which accepted an experiential faith based on "tongue speaking," visions and feeling followed Sidney Rigdon into Mormonism. It is but a short step from an experiential faith based on subjective experience into the acceptance of latter-day revelation like the Book of Mormon.*

> *The whole of Mormonism, with its book of "latter-day revelations," its priesthood and necessarily attending phenomena, is but one of several such developments in the history claiming supernatural gifts and Holy Spirit direction.*

> *Accepting as fact that such charismatic gifts are of divine origin and genuine in these modern movements, one would have no choice but to accept the claims and doctrines of each. Each presents its case as validly as the other.*[4]

An appeal to personal experience is not adequate. All sincere people believe they are religiously right. Paul did when he persecuted the church.[5]

Buddhists, Moslems, Spiritualists and Pagans all believe they are right. Ecstatic utterances are know in all these religions and are thought to be evidence of Divine sanction,

4. R. L. Roberts, "Mormonism—An Example of Experiential Religion," The Star, 1:71 (January, 1971), p. 7.
5. Acts 23:1.

but such phychological experiences do not guarantee that a religion is from God.

Personal subjective feelings and the physical phenomenon that accompany them do not provide an adequate standard for faith. One's interpretation of these feelings may be false. The result would be believing a lie. The New Testament teaches that there will always be false prophets.[6] For this reason John says that spirits are to be tested to see if they are from God.[7] False teachers are often very sincere. They believe what they teach, but they teach error. They not only deceive others; they also deceive themselves. Paul tells of such men: *"And for this cause God sendeth them a working of error, that they should believe a lie: that they all might be judged who believed not the truth, but had pleasure in unrighteousness."*[8]

The logical consequences of accepting glossolalia as a Divine gift nullifies the sufficiency of the Scriptures. The same kind of arguments that are made for glossolalia are also made for latter-day revelation. The personal subjective nature of glossolalia makes it logically impossible for its advocates to demand the objective standard of the Scriptures as authority in religion.

The Question of Spiritual Maturity

The question of spiritual maturity is also at the very heart of any discussion of glossolalia. Advocates of glossolalia believe the experience adds to their spiritual maturity. After the experience, they look back on their former life as spiritually impoverished. They encourage others to seek the experience in order that they also can know the spiritual abundance that they now possess. They look condescending upon those who

6. II Peter 2:1.
7. I John 4:1.
8. II Thessalonians 2:11-12.

question the validity of the experience by such declarations as, "If you ain't tried it, don't knock it."

It is perhaps significant that spiritual maturity was a point discussed by Paul when he wrote to correct the abuse of the *glossa* gift at Corinth. He did not suggest that those who were exercising the *glossa* gift were spiritually mature. They were not. In abusing the gift they were causing schisms in the body.[9] They were neglecting or at least placing the permanent gifts of faith, hope and love in a secondary position.[10] They were causing confusion in the assembly.[11] They were so wrapped up with their own gift that they did not care whether it edified the church.[12] Paul admonished those who were abusing the *glossa* gift to put away childish things [13] and not to be children in mind.[14] The word *teleion* which is translated "perfect" in 13:10 and "men" in 14:20 must be understood as that which is mature or has come to full age.

Paul is saying in I Corinthians 13:10 when that which is perfect (*teleion*—mature) is come, there will be no need for the gifts of wisdom, tongues and knowledge. He is saying in I Corinthians 14:20 that those who thought tongues were greater than prophecy and were using them without an interpreter were childish. They needed to grow up and be men (*teleion*—mature).

The *glossa* gift at Corinth is not the same·thing as contemporary glossolalia. [15] It appears, however, that both those who abused the *glossa* gift at Corinth and contemporary glossolalists

9. I Corinthians 12:21-25.
10. I Corinthians 12:31; 13:3.
11. I Corinthians 14:23-26.
12. I Corinthians 14:1-19.
13. I Corinthians 13:11.
14. I Corinthians 14:20.
15. See page 57ff.

are mistaken about their spiritual maturity. Paul showed that those who abused the *glossa* gift at Corinth were immature. Perhaps the following points will point out some of the immaturity that exists among the advocates of glossolalia.

Glossolalia is not a mark of spirituality, but a sign of self-centeredness. It causes a person to focus upon himself rather than others. To illustrate this point this author opened a journal and read the testimony of one who claimed a religious experience—including glossolalia. He claimed that the experience made him more spiritual; yet, the first person is used twenty-four times in three short paragraphs.

You never find a Spirit-filled person in the Scriptures saying "I am filled with the Holy Spirit." Neither do you find one boasting of " speaking in tongues." Paul did say, "I speak with tongues more than you all."[16] He was not boasting of the gift in this passage but showing the Corinthians that his criticism of their abuse of the gifts was not motivated by jealousy. He speaks of his own *glossa* gift only to show that it was useless in edifying the church.

Spirit-filled Christians in the New Testament did not have to advertise that the Holy Spirit was dwelling in them. This conclusion was either noted by their hearers or recorded by others. Christians in New Testament times did not take time to dwell on their own feelings. Their primary concern was for others.

A person who has been saved by the grace of God and has received the gift of the Holy Spirit has little time left for introversion.

The test of a man's spirituality is not an emotional high. The same thing can be accomplished with drugs. The test of a

16. I Corinthians 14:18.

man's spirituality is his devotion to God and his service to man. Jesus' great commandment was to love God and love one's neighbor. He did not say anything about falling in love with one's own feelings.

Certainly there are spirit-filled men and women today. Every Christian has the Holy Spirit dwelling in him. The presence of the Holy Spirit is not shown by ecstatic utterances but by the fruit of the Spirit. This includes love, joy, peace, long-suffering, kindness, goodness, faithfulness, meekness and self-control.[17]

Glossolalia is not a sign of Divine favor but is often found to be a temptation to human pride. Certainly it inflates the ego to think that one has been picked by God to receive a special gift. One writer has observed:

> *The speaking in tongues is an end within itself, its very unintelligibility satisfying the psychological craving for extraordinary expression and religious craving for proof of inspiration and the direct action of God.*[18]

Bultmann suggests that one of the basic errors that Paul sought to correct in the church at Corinth was Gnosticism. He writes:

> *Already at Corinth there had been a movement of Gnostic pneumatics, and Paul had to resist their influence. The struggle for speculative wisdom (I Corinthians 1: 17ff), the insistence on gnosis, on the exousia with which it invested them in matters of personal conduct (6:12ff.; 8:1ff.), and on demonstrations of a pneumatic quality (II Corinthians 10-13), shows that the opponents were Gnostics; so, too, does the tendency toward asceticism*

17. Galatians 5:22-23.
18. George Barton Cutten, Speaking with Tongues (New Haven: Yale University Press, 1927), p. 182.

(I Corinthians 7) and the denial of the resurrection of the body (I Corinthians 15). [19]

Bultmann particularly sees Gnosticism in I Corinthians 13. Those who had spiritual gifts at Corinth —including the *glossa* gift—only were able to know in part.[20] Knowledge (*gnōsis*) shall be done away.[21] All knowledge (*gnōsis*) without love is nothing.[22] It seemed that those who were abusing the *glossa* gift at Corinth were also involved in Gnosticism.

A basic concept of Gnosticism was that man could know God by direct subjective knowledge. This made objective revelation of God in Christ and the Scriptures unnecessary. This made obedience to commandments and demonstrated love unnecessary. The Gnostics sought to know God through subjective experience.[23] They had gone beyond the historical Jesus who came in the flesh and his objective teachings.[24]

The contemporary doctrine and practice of glossolalia touches ancient Gnosticism in a number of ways. Adherents of both seek to be the spiritual elite. Adherents of both play down objective revelation and exalt personal subjective experience. Adherents of both emphasize subjective love and de-emphasize objective commandment keeping. The early church refuted Gnosticism. Much of the New Testament was written to refute their errors. The same passages which refuted their errors will also refute contemporary glossolalia as being from God.

19. Rudolf Bultmann, "Ginoskō," Theological Dictionary of the New Testament edited by Gerhard Kittel, Vol. 1. (Grand Rapids: Wm. E. Eerdmans, 1964), p. 709.

20. I Corinthians 13:8.

21. Ibid.

22. I Corinthians 13:2.

23. Bultmann, op. cit., pp. 711-13.

24. II John 7-11.

Both the ancient Gnostics and contemporary glossolalists rely on existential experiences as evidence of knowing Jesus. John says, *"Hereby we know that we know him, if we keep his commandments. He that saith, I know him, and keepeth not his commandments, is a liar and the truth is not in him."*[25] It is not subjective experiences, but simple obedience to the objective word that is evidence of fellowship with Jesus. It was true then, and it is true today.

Both the ancient Gnostics and contemporary glossolalists claim secret knowledge or new personal revelation. Both believe that their faith is not based merely upon the historical Jesus and his objective teachings revealed in the Scriptures. They both seek personal subjective knowledge that goes beyond Jesus and his teaching which is in the Scriptures. John says, *"Believe not every spirit, but prove the spirits, whether they are of God; because many false prophets are gone out into the world."*[26] John further warns in his second epistle:

Whosoever goeth onward and abideth not in the teaching of Christ, hath not God; he that abideth in the teaching, the same hath both the Father and the Son. If any one cometh unto you, and bringeth not this teaching, receive him not into your house, and give him no greeting for he that giveth him greeting partaketh in his evil works.[27]

Both the ancient Gnostics and contemporary glossolalists depart from the fellowship of other Christians because they feel spiritually superior. They feel the fellowship of other Christians and the practical love of the brethren unimportant after they have arrived to the spiritual heights of direct communion with God. John says, *"They went out from us but they were not of us; for if they had been of us, they would*

25. I John 2:3-4.
26. I John 4:1.
27. II John 9-11.

*have continued with us, but they went out that they might be
made manifest that they all are not of us.*"[28] He also says, *"If
a man says, I love God and hateth his brother, he is a liar."*[29]
John warns the Gnostics, who felt they were superior to the
fellowship of other Christians and above sin, that they were in
danger of losing the effects of the blood of Christ. He says:

> *If we walk in the light, as he is in the light, we have fel-
> lowship one with another, and the blood of Jesus his
> Son cleanseth us from all sin. If we say that we have no
> sin, we deceive ourselves, and the truth is not in us.*[30]

Glossolalia is not a sign of faith but a symptom of doubt.
When men seek supernatural events to strengthen their faith,
to confirm their salvation and to direct their lives, it demon-
strates a lack of confidence in that which God has said in the
Scriptures. This shows why Jesus refused the temptation of
the devil. He did not need a sign to see if God would keep his
promise.[31] Jesus' faith in God, his promises and the Scriptures did not need to be propped up with a sign. The Pharisee s
often asked Jesus for a sign.[32] Jesus rebuked them for seeking
signs. He said, *"An evil and adulterous generation seeketh after
a sign."*[33] They even asked for Jesus to come down from the
cross so they could believe.[34]

The statement that Abraham made to the rich man in Hades
applies in such a situation. *"If they hear not Moses and the
prophets, neither will they be persuaded if one rise from the
dead."*[35] The Scriptures are sufficient to produce faith. No

---

28. I John 2:19.
29. I John 4:20.
30. I John 1:7-8.
31. Matthew 4:6-7.
32. Matthew 12:38ff; 16:1-4; Luke 11:14-16; John 2:18-22; 6:30-35
33. Matthew 12:39.
34. Matthew 27:42.
35. Luke 16:31.

other signs are needed. To ask for signs when God has already given evidence in the Scriptures is to make trial of the Lord.

Faith that comes from a psychological experience will die when the psychological experience is understood. Faith that comes from a feeling of elation will die when there are feelings of depression. Faith that comes as a result of viewing something considered miraculous will die when it is shown to be a fraud. But faith that comes by hearing the word of God will always endure.

One who knows Jesus does not need his religions propped up by the psychological experience of glossolalia. Faith that comes by a reasonable study of the Word of God is not to be cast aside for the bubble of emotional subjectivism. One who has heard the call of Jesus Christ will not be listening for other voices from the unknown.

A Christian lives in the real world of service, devotion, evangelism, benevolence and morality. Psuedo-religious, self-centered, psychological experiences find no place in his life. Such are signs of an immature faith and an impoverished spirituality. Seeking such experiences is vain and foolish. It is like chasing the wind.

Men do not run after mirages who dwell in the oasis of God. Men do not grab for straws in the water who are already safe in the ship of God.

Problems of Glossolalia

If one accepts glossolalia as being a gift from God—the *glossa* gift of the New Testament—he is faced with numerous insurmountable problems. These problems must be faced. They must be answered in the light of the Scriptures and reason. It is not sufficient to drown them out by enthusiastic testimony. It is not sufficient to ignore them or pass over them lightly as if they were of no consequence. It is not sufficient to answer them by personal subjective feeling.

There are three assumptions which must be made in accepting contemporary glossolalia as the *glossa* gift of the New Testament.

(1)   It is assumed that the glossolalia experience is from God. It can not be proved either by Scripture or reason. This is quite an assumption since the New Testament says that the *glossa* gift was to cease of itself. And that the seducing spirits would continue in the latter times and the man of sin would be working signs and lying wonders through the power of Satan.[36] A sobering passage for all who claim the power of supernatural signs today is Matthew 7:22-23. The scene is the judgment. The judge is Jesus. The ones being judged are those who in the name of Jesus did many mighty works—including the miraculous. Hear their testimony: *"Lord, Lord, did we not prophesy by thy name, and by thy name cast out demons, and by thy name do many mighty works?"* Now hear their judgment: *"And then will I profess unto them, I never knew you: depart from me, ye that work iniquity."* Not all spiritual experiences, wonders and signs are from God. Some are from the devil. False prophets work signs.[37]   Not all spirits are from God.[38] There are unholy spirits as well as the Holy Spirit. When the New Testament discusses signs in the last times, it usually attributes them to the forces of evil.[39]

(2) It is generally assumed that contemporary glossolalia is

36. I Timothy 4:1; II Thessalonians 2:8-9.
37. Matthew 24:24.
38. I John 4;1.
39. II Corinthians 11:13-15; II Timothy 3:13; Revelations 13:11-14; 16:13-14; 19 20.

language.[40]   This has not and can not be demonstrated.
Controlled studies such as have been done by E. Mansell
Pattison furnish ample evidence that none of the numerous
subjects represented in their studies spoke in language unknown to them.[41]

(3)   It is assumed that contemporary glossolalia is the
same as the New Testament *glossa* gift.   It has already been
shown that this could not be the case.[42]   Advocates of glossolalia must go outside of the New Testament to find support
for it.   One must not accept a doctrine and practice and then
try to read it back into the New Testament text.   This is
eisegesis, not exegesis.   One must not wrest the Scriptures.

If any one of these assumptions breaks down, the whole
doctrine and practice of glossolalia is without authority.   Since
none of these assumptions can be proved either by Scripture or
reason, there can not be any Scriptural or reasonable justifica-
tion for it.

The glossolalist is confronted by numerous dilemmas which
should cause him to do some soul searching to see if his experience is from God or man.

If glossolalia is devotional language which is not understood
by the speaker, (1) How can one really know if he is praising
God or cursing God by these utterances? (2) How can he know
if his speech comes from God or the devil? (3) How can he be

40. Glossolalists differ greatly on just what kind of language it is.
There are some who understand it as ecstatic utterance, but the majority
believe it to be languages.
41. E. Mansell Pattison, "Behavioral Science Research on the Nature
of Glossolalia," Journal of American Scientific Affiliation 20:3 (September, 1978), p. 73ff.
42. See page 35-45.

sure it is not a psychological experience arising from his own subconscious? The very unintelligibility of the utterance keeps one from having any valid criteria to judge these things.

If glossolalia is real experience from God: (1) How can the same phenomenon in world religions, ancient and modern, be explained? (2) How can one explain the same phenomenon found in psychological studies completely outside of the religious context? (3) How can one account for the conflicting doctrines and practices among the different advocates of glossolalia? (4) How can one logically reject latter-day revelations such as the Book of Mormon? One can not escape this dilemma by appealing to subjective experience or denying that such dilemma exists.

If contemporary glossolalia is the same as the New Testament *glossa* gift: (1) Why is it not used as was the New Testament gift to speak to every man in the language wherein he was born? (2) Why is it exalted to a prominent position in teaching and practice instead of restrained and limited as was the New Testament gift? (3) Why is it not like the undeniable signs of the New Testament?[43]

Faith in Jesus Christ does not throw reason out the door. Reason complements faith. The God who made order out of confusion—*kosmos* out of chaos—in creation certainly is not the author of confusion in the faith and practice of Christians—his new creation.

43. Acts 4:16.

CHAPTER 13

PRACTICAL CONSIDERATIONS

The glossolalia issue is more than an academic study. It is a live issue touching the lives of numerous Christians and presenting problems in scores of churches in all parts of the world. What is to be done about it?

It can not be ignored. Its advocates are evangelistic. The very nature of the phenomenon is such that it rushes into the vacuum caused by a secular age and the void found in unspiritual churches. The first step in solving a problem is facing up to the reality of the problem and its causes. Church leaders can not hide their heads in the sand and hope that the problem will go away. They must solve the problem and correct the causes that produced it. It must not be regarded as innocent babblings of immature Christians. It is a dangerous delusion. It arises from man's own subconscious and is used by the devil as a substitute for faithful service and genuine spirituality.

Many religious leaders would view this as only an insignificant matter of opinion and tolerate it. This toleration allows time for its advocates to permeate the total membership with this practice. Some will espouse it. Then small prayer groups and home studies will start collecting those who are in sympathy with the practice. Finally, a schism will come. The schism will not necessarily be the result of devisive planning on the part of the advocates of glossolalia. It will come because two conflicting concepts of authority can not exist in one unified body. When one group holds to subjective prompting of the "spirit" and the other group holds to the objective teachings of the Scripture, a clash must ultimately come. This is not to say that either group planned it that way. It happens because they hold to conflicting doctrines.

Four Suggestions to Church Leaders

Four basic things are suggested to church leaders as they attempt to deal with this problem on the congregational level.

First, they must try to understand some of the causes which have produced the psychological need for glossolalia. They need also to understand what those caught up in the movement are saying, Both are difficult. The causes which produced the phenomenon may vary from place to place. It is difficult to understand what the glossolalists are saying since they do not speak the same thing.

The problem can not be permanently solved until the factors which caused the problem are corrected. Each congregation should take a hard look at what they are trying to do to promote spirituality among its members. It is a judgment upon those who lead in the church that those who follow their lead are so spiritually impoverished that they seek such counterfeits of the devil to fill their spiritual hunger. Is it because worship has become traditional and ritualistic? Is it because teachers have not made their lessons personal enough to apply in the everyday-work-a-day world? Is it because our preaching has emphasized guilt instead of forgiveness; fear instead of assurance; judgment instead of salvation? Is it because leaders of the church have put away their swords and reached a cease-fire agreement with false teachers. Uninformed souls without a knowledge of doctrine are unprepared to stand in the time of battle. Causes may vary, but dedicated and perceptive leaders in the church will seek to know the cause and correct it.

It would be well for all Christians to hear what some of the glossolalists are saying. Who will deny the need for exuberant and joyful Christian living? Such is emphasized among the glossolalists. Who can question the validity of emphasizing prayer and a study of the Scriptures? Who can criticize the emphasis they place on speaking of their faith at all times and in all places? It is a shame that sometimes one sees the very things that are emphasized by the glossolalists neglected in the life of the church.

Second, church leaders must lead in filling the void that too often is found in the spiritual life of Christians in a skeptical and secular age. This author firmly believes the best way to overcome the "tongue speaking" heresy within the church is to develop a greater spirituality in worship, service and fellowship. In fact this is the only way that it can be permanently overcome.

In the cases studied and experienced by this author, three things seem to keep arising: (1) The person did not have a full and meaningful spiritual life before he sought the glossolalia experience. They sometimes went through the mechanics of attending services and doing "church work" but there was no personal vital spiritual devotion. Think of the many ways the church should help one in such a situation (2) The person had severe personal conflicts with which he was wrestling. Financial problems, moral and ethical inconsistences and family tensions were a few of the conflicts. These conflicts often lead to despair until they were ready to seize anything that would promise help. Think of how the teaching and fellowship in the church should help to resolve these conflicts. (3) The person wanted to escape personal responsibility. If he were in sin, he did not want the responsibility of repentance and confession. This was too humiliating. Glossolalia promised an easier way out. If he were failing, he did not want to admit failure and accept the blame those with whom he associated. It was easier to try a new way with new people and lay the blame for his failures on the old way and his old associates. He could not face the responsibility of his own failure so he did a spiritual cop out.

Teaching on the Holy Spirit has been neglected in the church. Perhaps the church is reaping the fruits of glossolalia because its teachers have neglected to sow the Biblical teachings concerning the Holy Spirit. When the Christian understands and appropriates the indwellings of the Holy Spirit,[1] His help in prayer,[2] and His work in producing the fruits of the Spirit,[3] he will not be tempted to follow the mirages of ecstasy. The church is suffering from a vacuum of teaching on the Holy Spirit. Where truth is not advocated, error is sure to rise. Many of those who have gone out from the church say that they had been taught that the Holy Spirit does not personally dwell in the Christian and that He is referred to as "it." This may be so in some places and at some times, but this author has not found such to be a prominent teaching where he has lived and worked. He has found, however, a great neglect of teaching on the doctrine of the Holy Spirit.

Church leaders ought to seek to make the practice of Christianity more personal and vital among the members of the church. Christians need to learn to speak of Jesus without hesitancy. They ought to be able to share with others the joy that Christ has brought to their lives in every-day language and in every-day situations. Christians should be able to talk of their spiritual needs to one another without embarrassment. Deep personal needs of a Chrsitian should be discussed from the pulpit along with doctrinal propositions and ecclesiastical promotion. Confession of sins and prayer for one another

1. I Corinthians 6:19.
2. Romans 8:26.
3. Galatians 5:22.

ought to be commonplace in the church. Perhaps it is the void that is caused by the lack of these things that has caused some to seek spiritual fulfillment in glossolalia.

Third, church leaders must be able to give a Scriptural refutation of the glossolalia doctrine and practice. It is not sufficient to make a dogmatic assertion that the doctrine is erroneous. One must be able to declare why it is in error. The practice can not be excluded from the church on the basis of tradition. It is not to be rejected just because it is different. Something different would be refreshing if it were closer to the Biblical pattern and had Scriptural authority. Church leaders must be able to refute glossolalia on the basis of Scripture and reason.

One must understand that the glossolalia practice is not wrong of itself. It is merely a psychological phenomenon. When it is understood as such, there is no spiritual harm in it. The error comes when it is believed to be a miraculous gift of God. It is not the phenomenon that is wrong. Its interpretation as a special gift of God is the error. The practice of glossolalia is not wrong of itself. Perhaps there are certain situations in which it could be helpful like drugs, hypnotism and shock treatments. It is the practice of glossolalia as a religious exercise which promotes confusion and schism in the body of Christ.

The author counselled with a lady for an extended period of time that practiced automatic writing[4] –a phenomenon similar to glossolalia. There were deep seated psychological reasons for her engaging in this practice. There was nothing wrong

4. Automatic writing is a phenomenon very similar to glossolalia – automatic speech. The hand writes without the conscious mind knowing what is being written. The movement is directed from the unconscious. This automatic writing generally is unintelligible scribbling. Sometimes words and phrases can be determined and be interpreted for therapeutic purposes.

with the practice as long as she understood that it was an extension of her own unconsciousness. In fact, it seemed in her case to relieve certain tensions and conflicts within her. The practice was a symptom of instability—but not wrong. If such automatic writing were to be interpreted as being a miraculous gift of God and used as a spiritual exercise, it would be erroneous.

In refuting the glossolalia error, one must draw the battle lines in the right place. There is no quarrel with the phenomenon itself. It is a psychological problem. The error comes with its interpretation as a Divine gift and its practice as a religious exercise.

In the refutation of glossolalia, one must avoid "scare tactics." Certainly it is a serious problem. Many excesses exist in certain cases. Sometimes moral problems are connected with its practice. Sometimes it is used to take advantage of the unlearned. The same things can be said about religion in general. Yet the excesses, abuses and the hypocrisy does not invalidate all religion. One must not attack glossolalia because of other unrelated problems found among its adherents.[5] The doctrine and practice itself must be refuted.

In the refutation of glossolalia one must not allow his polemics to get in the way of exegesis. Scriptural refutation must never divorce a passage from its context. One must not place a strain on the passage in order to make it fit his argument. This is always difficult to do. It is doubtful that if any person ever fully succeeds in being this objective. Yet this is the ideal. When poor exegesis is used or an invalid argument is put forth, it weakens the case for truth.

5. It should be observed that the surrender of the will that takes place in the glossolalia experience along with the high emotional involvement makes its advocate highly susceptible to such problems.

There is ample evidence to show that the doctrine and practice of glossolalia is not from God. This is sufficient. Church leaders should take a positive stand and lead the church away from this counterfeit into real spiritual maturity in Christ.

Fourth, church leaders must attempt to restore the erring. In spite of all that the leaders of the church can do, some will be led into error. Church leaders might provide excellent spiritual leadership and be able to refute glossolalia very well by Scripture and reason and still some will be led into error. Even among Jesus' twelve apostles there was a Judas.

What is to be done when one becomes involved in glossolalia? How are the leaders of the church to react? First, they must teach and exhort those who are in sympathy with it so they will not be lost through neglect. [6] Second, they are to reprove, rebuke and restore those who have espoused it. [7] In so doing you will save a soul from death. [8] Third, those who are rebellious and teach the false doctrine and promote schism in the body of Christ are to be disciplined—even to the withdrawal of fellowship. [9] Only in this way can their souls ultimately be saved and the purity of the church be maintained.

Some Conclusions

The author has attempted to draw the following conclusions from the study of the material in this book.

(1) The New Testament *glossa* gift is to be understood as being the ability to speak in foreign languages. It is to be so regarded in Corinth as well as Jerusalem. There is the possibility that some at Corinth were trying to counterfeit the real gift

6. Hebrews 3:13.
7. II Timothy 4:2-4; Titus 1:11; Galatians 6:1.
8. James 5:19-20.
9. II John 9: Romans 16:17.

by substituting the ecstatic utterances of the pagan cults—even to saying that Jesus was anathema. This phenomenon was not the *glossa* gift but came from another spirit.

(2)   The *glossa* gift in the New Testament was received through the baptism of the Holy Spirit and the laying on of the apostles' hands. Its purpose was to confirm the men and the message of God.

(3)   Contemporary glossolalia is a psychological phenomenon common to all religions, ancient and modern. It is to be found in contemporary world religions, Spiritualism and sometimes completely outside the religious context.

(4)   The present practice of glossolalia has no support from the New Testament. The New Testament does predict signs of the devil which would deceive people in the latter times.

(5)   The logical consequence of glossolalia is the denial of the objective authority of Jesus Christ as revealed in the Scriptures. The assumptions which allow glossolalia also allow for latter-day revelation such as the Book of Mormon.

(6)   Glossolalia is not a sign of Divine favor and spirituality, but the fruit of self-centeredness, pride, doubt and immaturity.

(7)   Glossolalia of itself is no more than a psychological phenomenon and is not wrong within itself. It becomes error when the experience is attributed to God, received as a miraculous gift and practiced as a religious exercise.

The author's conclusion is that GLOSSOLALIA IS NOT FROM GOD, BUT FROM MAN.

First Printing, February, 1971 (8,000 copies)
Second Printing, November, 1972 (6,000 copies)

SCRIPTURE INDEX
GLOSSOLALIA